Street by Street

BASINGSTOKE

ALTON, ANDOVER, FLEET

Bramley, Chineham, Hartley Wintney, Hook, Kingsclere, Oakley, Odiham, Overton, Tadley, Whitchurch

G000067104

Ist edition May 2001

© Automobile Association Developments Limited 2001

This product includes map data licensed from Ordnance Survey® with the permission of the Controller of Her Majesty's Stationery Office. © Crown copyright 2000. All rights reserved. Licence No: 399221.

Published by AA Publishing (a trading name of Automobile Association Developments Limited, whose registered office is Norfolk House, Priestley Road, Basingstoke, Hampshire, RG24 9NY. Registered number 1878835).

Mapping produced by the Cartographic Department of The Automobile Association.

ISBN 0 7495 2617 3

A CIP Catalogue record for this book is available from the British Library.

Printed by Edicoes ASA, Oporto, Portugal

Ref: ML001

Enlarged scale pages 1:10,000 6.3 inches to 1 mile

miles
0 — 1/4 — 1/2

kilometres
0 — 1/4 — 1/2 — 3/4 — 1

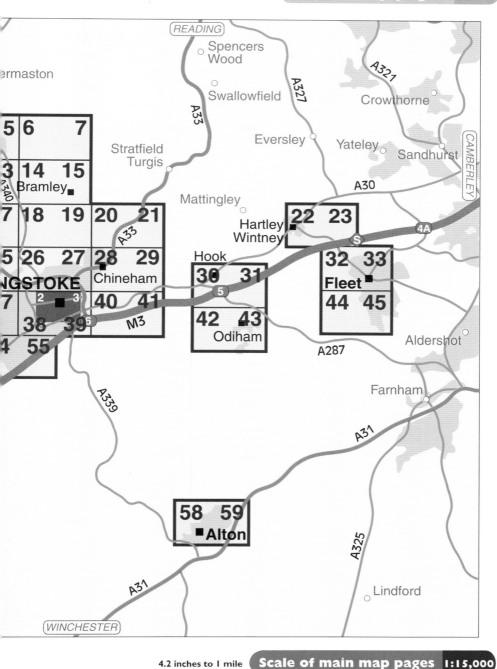

ermaston

READING

Spencers
Wood

Swallowfield

A327

A321

Crowthorne

| 5 | 6 | | 7 |
| 3 | 14 | 15 | |

Bramley

Stratfield
Turgis

A33

Eversley

Yateley

Sandhurst

CAMBERLEY

A30

| 7 | 18 | 19 | 20 | 21 |

Mattingley

A33

| 22 | 23 |

Hartley
Wintney

4A

S

| 5 | 26 | 27 | 28 | 29 |

Hook

NGSTOKE

Chineham

| 30 | 31 |

5

| 32 | 33 |

Fleet

| 7 | 2 | 3 | 40 | 41 |
| | 38 | 39 | | |

M3

| 42 | 43 |

Odiham

| 44 | 45 |

6

| 4 | 55 |

A287

Aldershot

A339

Farnham

A31

| 58 | 59 |

Alton

A325

A31

Lindford

WINCHESTER

4.2 inches to 1 mile **Scale of main map pages** **1:15,000**

| 0 | 1/4 | miles | 1/2 | 3/4 | 1 |

| 0 | 1/4 | 1/2 | kilometres 3/4 | 1 | 1 1/4 | 1 1/2 |

Junction 9	Motorway & junction
Services	Motorway service area
	Primary road single/dual carriageway
Services	Primary road service area
	A road single/dual carriageway
	B road single/dual carriageway
	Other road single/dual carriageway
	Restricted road
	Private road
←	One way street
	Pedestrian street
	Track/ footpath
	Road under construction
	Road tunnel
P	Parking

P+	Park & Ride
	Bus/Coach station
	Railway & main railway station
	Railway & minor railway station
⊖	Underground station
⊖	Light Railway & station
++++++++	Preserved private railway
LC	Level crossing
•—•—•—•	Tramway
----------	Ferry route
....	Airport runway
— · — · — · —	Boundaries- borough/ district
▼▼▼▼▼▼▼	Mounds
93	Page continuation 1:15,000
7	Page continuation to enlarged scale 1:10,000

	River/canal, lake, pier		Toilet with disabled facilities
	Aqueduct, lock, weir		Petrol station
465 ▲ Winter Hill	Peak (with height in metres)	**PH**	Public house
	Beach	**PO**	Post Office
	Coniferous woodland		Public library
	Broadleaved woodland	*i*	Tourist Information Centre
	Mixed woodland		Castle
	Park		Historic house/ building
	Cemetery	Wakehurst Place NT	National Trust property
	Built-up area	**M**	Museum/ art gallery
	Featured building	†	Church/chapel
⊓⊔⊓⊔⊓⊔	City wall		Country park
A&E	Accident & Emergency hospital		Theatre/ performing arts
	Toilet		Cinema

F G H J **27** J K

Arlott Dr
Baynard Cl
Lefroy Avenue
Westray Close
Pemerton Rd
Lewis Dr
Norn Hill Cl
Gordon Cl
Gresley Road
A339
Bell Road
Industrial Estate

Shooters
Avenue
Norn Hill Cl
The Laurels
Bell Road
Gresley Road

Mary Way
Warton Rd
Doswell Way
Coronation Road
Daneshill East
Industrial Estate

Lyford Road
Doswell Way
Gresley Road
PO
P+train
Cowdrey Hei
B

Deane's
The AA -
Fanum House
2

P
Burnian
Basing View
A339

Alencon Link
Old Reading Road
Basing View
Basing View
EAST A3010
WAY
3

P
Basing View
Basingstoke
County Court
Police Station
EAST
WAY
A3010

WAY A3010
EASTROP
ROUNDABOUT
CHURCHILL WAY
Eastrop Park
4

RG21
Bus Station
Timberlake Road
Eastrop Way
Eastrop Way
Water Way
39

St Mary's
Eastfield Av
Blackwater Cl
Weysprings Close
Frome Cl
Lune
Buckby La
The Butty
Barbel Av
The Rushes

Goat Lane
Eastrop
Eastfield Av
Allnutt Av
Loddon
Reading Cl
Neath Rd
Thames
Lune Ct
Dr
Medway
Duddon Way
Damsel Pth
Waterlily Cl

New Road
Seal Rd
Chequers Rd
Surrey Hants
Borders NHS
Trust
Ribble Way
Irwell Cl
Test
Rothay Cl
Hamble Ct
Duddon Way
Severn Way

Hampshire
County Council
The
Business Centre
Lytton
Colne Way
Kennet Cl
London Road
Hotel

P
Red Lion La
Magistrates
Court
London Road
Eastrop
Old Common Road
A30
5

Willis
Mus
Feathers
May Pl
White Hart Lane
Harriet
Costello
School
Hotel
Dam
Turner Cl
Hogarth Cl
Way

PO
Anchor Yard
Civic
Offices
Turner Cl
Turner Cl
6

Road
Basingstoke &
Deane Borough
Council Offices
Van Dyck Cl
Van Dyck Way

Bandstand
John Arlott
Pavilion
Reynolds Cl
Raphael Cl
Van Dyck Close
Ruskin Cl
7

nsfield Road
Hackwood Road
War
Memorial
Park
P
Rembrandt
Close
School
Black Dam Way

School
Montague Place
HACKWOOD ROAD
ROUNDABOUT
RINGWAY
**Black
Dam**

Cliddesden Road
Applegarth
Hampshire
County Council
Crossborough Hill
Park Gdns
Park Gdns
Whistle Cl
Holbein Close
Renoir Close
Constable Cl

Russell Road
Howard Rd
HACKWOOD ROAD
Chesterfield Rd
Westfield Rd
Grove Road
39
Black Dam Way
Jennings
PO

St Marys
e
Camrose Wy
Camfield Close
Grove Road
Windser Way

F G H **39** J K

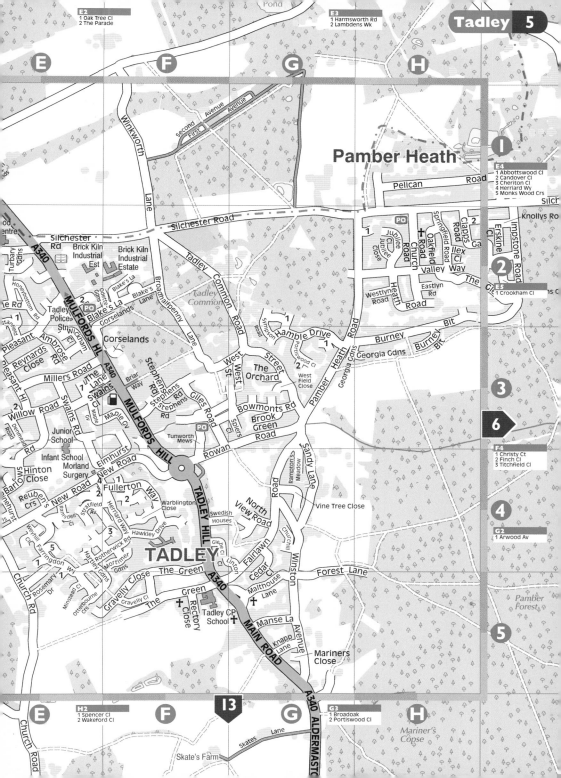

E2
1 Oak Tree Cl
2 The Parade

E3
1 Harmsworth Rd
2 Lambdens Wk

E   F   G   H

Pamber Heath

Pelican   Road

silch

I

E4
1 Abbottswood Cl
2 Candover Cl
3 Cheriton Cl
4 Herriard Wy
5 Monks Wood Crs

Second Avenue
First Avenue
Winkworth Lane

Silchester Road

Knollys Ro

PO

Jubilee Close
Jubilee Close
Oakfield Road
Springfield Road
Clapps Road
Erskine
Impstone Road
Ga

Silchester Rd

Brick Kiln Industrial Est

Brick Kiln Industrial Estate

Church Road
Valley Way
Ilex Cl

The

2

E5
1 Crookham Cl

ns

Tadley Common

Tadley Common Road

Blake's La
Blake's Lane

Odell's Gdns
Gorselands

Westlynn Road
Heath Road
Eastlyn Rd

Bit

A340

Turbary
Stanfield

Holyebourne Rd

le Rd

Silchester Rd

Tadley Police Stn

PO

Wickham La

Gorselands

Affpenny Lane
Broad

Symson

Hamble Drive

Portswood Cl

Pamber Heath Road

Burney
Georgia Gdns
Burney Bit

3

Pleasant
Reynards Close
Ambrose Rd

Millers Road

The Lane

Swains Rd

MULFORDS HILL

A340

Stephens Rd

Briar Way

Stephens Rd
Stephens Rd

West St
West St

The Orchard

Street
West

West Field Close

Georgia Gdns

6

F4
1 Christy Ct
2 Finch Cl
3 Titchfield Cl

Pleasant H

Willow Road

Swains Road

Denmead Rd

Maple Ct

Maj Ct

Giles Road
Spiers

Bowmonts Rd

Brook Green Road

4

G2
1 Arwood Av

Junior School

Elmhurst

New Road

Tunworth Mews

PO

Rowan

Sandy Lane

Rampton's Meadow

Church Road

Vine Tree Close

Infant School
Morland Surgery
Hinton Close

Reuben's Crs
Spatfield Av
Ramsdell Cl
Herriard Way

Fullerton Way

Warblington Close

Swedish Houses

North View Road

Road

Forest Lane

5

G3
1 Broadoak
2 Portiswood Cl

Barlo
Weyhill

Farringdon Cl

Rotherwick Rd
Mortimer Gdns
Harley Gdns

Hawkley Drive

TADLEY

The Green

Gravelly Close

Church Rd
Rosemary Dr
Minstead Cl
Orterbourne Crs

Gravelly Cl

The Green

Glebe Cl

Linton

Fairlawn

Cedar Cl
Malthouse Lane

Winston Avenue

Mariners Close

Pamber Forest

Rectory Close

Tadley CP School

Manse La

Knapp Lane

MAIN ROAD

A340

E   F   I3   G   H

H2
1 Spencer Cl
2 Wakeford Cl

Mariner's Copse

Church Road

ALDERMASTO

Skates Lane

Skate's Farm

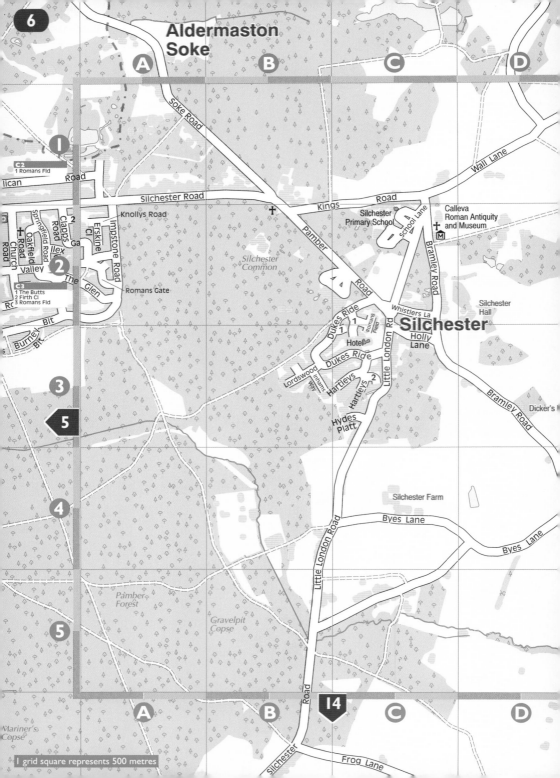

6

Aldermaston
Soke

A   **B**   **C**   **D**

I

C2
1 Romans Fld

lican   Road

Silchester Road

Wall Lane

Knollys Road

Kings   Road

Silchester
Primary School

School Lane

Calleva
Roman Antiquity
and Museum

M

Springfield Road

Clapps Ga

Erskine Cl

Impstone Road

Oakfield Road

Church Road

Valley

Ilex

The Glen

2

1 The Butts
2 Firth Cl
3 Romans Fld

C3

Romans Gate

Silchester
Common

Pamber

Road

Whistlers La

Silchester

Silchester
Hall

Dukes Ride

1

Romans Field

Hotel

Holly
Lane

Little London Rd

Burnel Blt

Blt

Rd

3

◀ **5**

Dukes Ride

Lordswood

Inhams Way

Hartleys

Hartleys

2

Hydes
Platt

Bramley Road

Dicker's

4

Silchester Farm

Byes   Lane

Byes   Lane

5

Pamber
Forest

Gravelpit
Copse

Little London Road

Mariner's
Copse

A   **B**   ▼ **I4**   **C**   **D**

Silchester Road

Frog Lane

I grid square represents 500 metres

Brocas Lands Farm

E F G H

Sheepgrove Farm

I

Wall Lane

✝

Church Lane

2

North Copse

Clappers Farm Rd

3

Brick

Lower Farm

4

Bramley Road

Three Ashes

5

Barefoot House

Haines Farm

E F **15** G H

ane

8

A B C D

Kisby's Farm

1

2

Mill
Lane

Oakfields
Close

Ecchinswell

Frobury Farm

White
Hill

3

4

Nuthanger Farm

5

Fossicks

A B C D

I grid square represents 500 metres

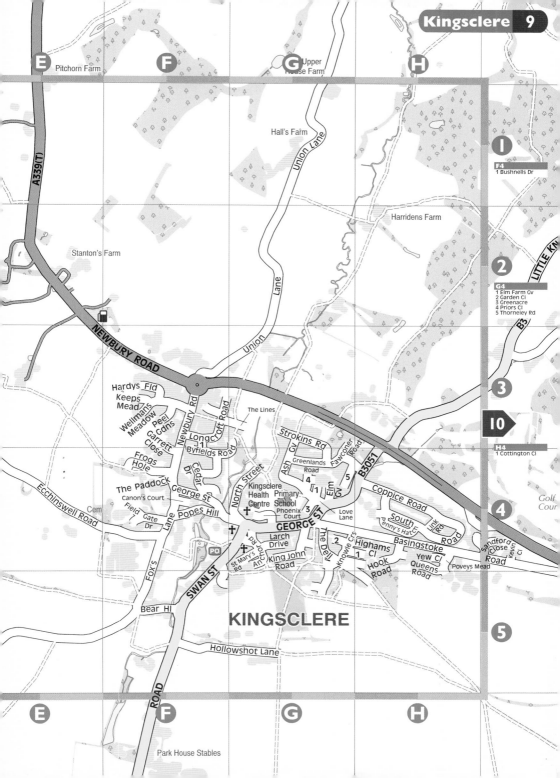

Hold

E F G H

Ham Lane

I

2

Wolverton Road

Ham Farm House

Ham

Lane

Chapel
Lane

Holt Lane

Wolverton Road

Brown's Farm

Po

**Wolverton
Common**

Baughurst House

3

Wolverton
Wood

12

**Towns
End**

Road

4

Ramsdell Road

ton House

**Stony
Heath**

5

Wolverton

Wolverton Lane

E F G H

Povey's Farm

Foscot Farm

12

A

B

4

C

D

Oak
House

Church

Church Brook Farm

I

2

Baughurst Road

†

Hillside

Brown's Farm

Baughurst House

3

II

Pound Green

**Browninghill
Green**

Stratton Manor

4

Hollybush Lane

5

Old Vyne
Lane

**Stony
Heath**

**West
Heath**

Povey's Farm

The Firs

A

B

16

C

D

Baughurst

White

1 grid square represents 500 metres

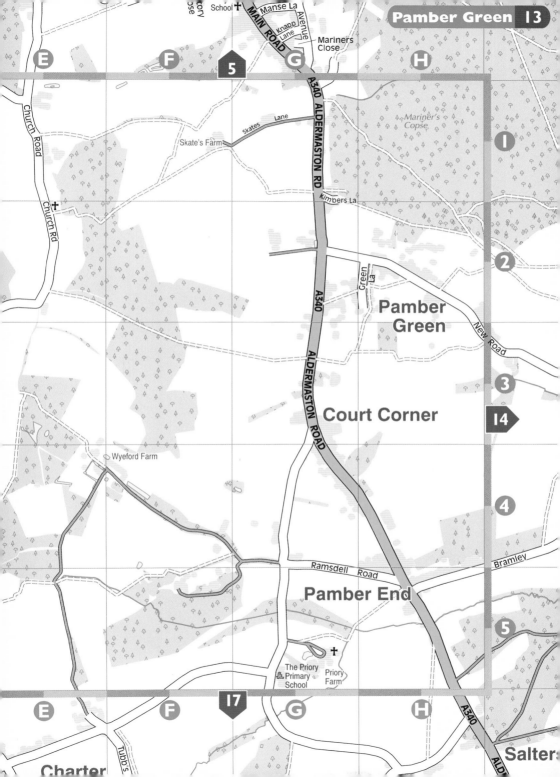

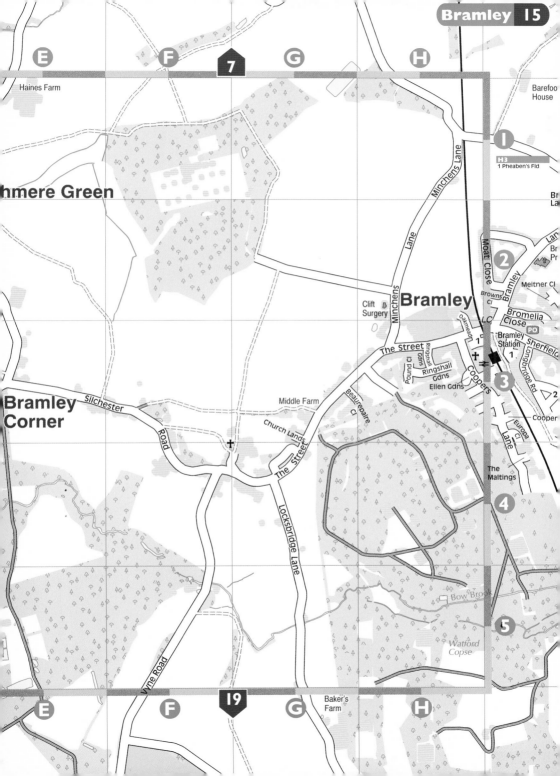

E
F
7
G
H

Haines Farm

Barefoo
House

hmere Green

Minchens Lane

1

H3
1 Pheaben's Fld

Br
La

Lane

Moat Close

2

Bramley

Meitner Cl

Minchens

Lane

Clift
Surgery

Bramley

Browns
Cl

Bromelia
Close

PO

LC

Bramley
Station

3

Sherfiel

The Street

Ringshall
Gdns

Oakmead

1

Coopers

Longbridge Rd

Pond Cl

Ringshall
Gdns

1

Silchester

Middle Farm

Church Lands

Beaurepaire
Cl

Ellen Gdns

Europa
Cl

**Bramley
Corner**

Road

The Street

Cooper

2

The Maltings

4

Locksbridge Lane

Bow Brook

5

Watford
Copse

Vyne Road

E
F
19
G
Baker's
Farm
H

16

Heath

Povey's Farm

A

B

12 Firs

C

West
Heath

D

Baughurst

Road

Monk

Sherborne

White

1

✝

Ramsdel

2

Ewhurst

Road

Skyer's Farm

Ewhurst Park

Sheepwash Lane

3

Skyer's
Wood

Basingstoke Road

4

Lloyd's Lane

Lower Farm

5

A

B

24

C

D

1 grid square represents 500 metres

E

F

13

G

H

†

iory
Primary
School

Priory
Farm

I Jalter

A340

ALDERMASTON ROAD

**Charter
Alley**

Tubb's

La

Rawlins Farm

2

Beal's Pightle

RG26

Salters Heath Road

3

18

*Privett
Copse*

Monk Sherborne

The Cl

Kiln

Lane

*Kiln
Green*

Salters ·

4

Weybroo

Salters · Heath Rd

5

†

Manor Farm

E

F

25

G

H

S

18

A B **14** C D

A340

Hill
End Farm

1 Salters Heath

ALDERMASTON ROAD

Beaurepaire
Farm

Cranes
Copse

Morgaston Road

2

Morgaston
Wood

3

◄**17**

4

West
End

Weybrook Ct

5

Cranes   Cranesfield
Spring   Rd
Ct

Cem

Vyne Meadow

Vyne Road

Spring Ct

Cranes
Bourne
Fld

Sherborne
St John
Primary School

A Sherborne St John **26**▼ C D

Spring Ct
The
Severals

Tyfield

PO
Kiln Road

Spencer's
Meadow

1 grid square represents 500 metres

Watford Copse

E

F

15

G

H

Vyne Road

Baker's Farm

I

Vyne Lodge Farm

Cufaude

2

Upper Cufaude Farm

Cufaude Lane

3

Vyne (NT)

20

Vyne Farm

4

Razor's Farm

Road

Crockford Lane

Tree Way

5

Achilles Cl

Renow

Maybrook

Marl's Lane

E

F

27

G

H

Hannore Rd

Mulber

Meadowland

Southlands

nfield

2

1

Oakwood

Aldenwood

Sorrell's Clos

Chineha

Whitewo

Martin

Wd

20

Watford Copse

A   B   C   D

1

Cufaude **2**

Upper Cufaude Farm

Cufaude Lane

Ragg Copse

Dixon Road

Sherfield Court

Ch

3

19

4

Razor's Farm

Sherfield Hall

Thyme Cl

Thyme Cl

Fennel Cl

Fennel

Belvedere Gdns

Foxs Furlong

Thornhill Way

Alax

Hanmore Road

Saffron Close

Juniper Cl

Juniper Cl

1

Stockbridge

4   3

Petersfie

5

Way

Tree

Lime

Achilles Cl

Renown Way

3

Petty's Brook Rd

Woodside Gdns

Bowman Road

Mongers Piece

4   2

Petersfie

Longstock Cl

Maybrook

Tangway

Forest Dr

Farm Rd

Guinea Ct

2

1

3

Thornhill

Toll

28

Lime

2

1

Alderford

Mulberry

Clibbons

Four Cl La

Thornhill Way

Adlington

Puttenham Rd

Cuffelle

Thornhill

St Leonard's Av

2

Lovegroves

Whitmarsh   Lane

A   B   C   D

Meadowland

Chineham

Sorrell's Close

St Gabriels

Kings

1 grid square represents 500 metres

E F G H I

Longbridge Cl

Willow

Bramley

Bow Gv

Carpenters

Poplar

Greenway

Poplar Road

Reading Road

✝ Sherfield
on Loddon

PO

Breach La

Pound
Meadow

Wildmoor La

A33

River Loddon

Mill Lane

E1
1 Bow Gdns
2 Goddards Cl

2

Mill F

Wildmoor Lane

North
Foreland Lodge

Lance Levy Farm

3

End

moor Lane

4

Su
Fa

Wildmoor Lane

Wildmoor

Ellis Farm

Lyde River

Moulshay Farm

5

29

E F G H

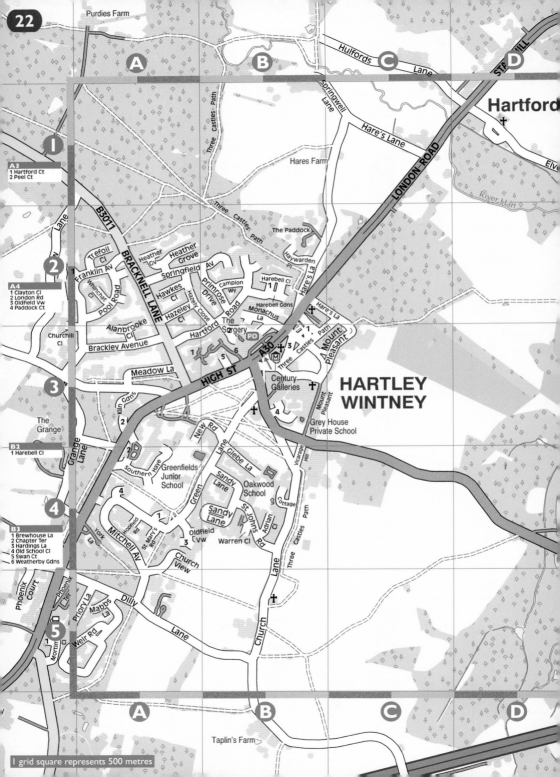

Star Hill
Plantation

Yateley
Heath
Wood

E **F** **G** **H**

Blackbushes Road

Ivyhole Hill

I

Lane

Home
Farm Rd

Elvetham Farm

Home Farm Road

2

Word
Hill Farm

Rotten Green Road

3

Elvetham
Hall

Turner's
Green Lane

P Lane

4

Turner's Green Lane

**Rotten
Green**

Elvetham

Street End

Pale Lane

Fleet Service Area

FLEET ROAD A323

5

E **F** **G** **H**

32

Palelane
Farm

E F 17 G H

Manor Farm

I

H5
1 Claudius Dr
2 Hadrians Wy

Field Barn Farm

Road

2

ALDERMASTON

A339(T)

KINGSCLERE

Rooksdown Lane

3

26

ROAD

Nightingale
Gdns
Florence
Wy
Gillies Dr

Barron Pl
Candel
Dr

Rooksdown Av

Mill Rd

Julius
Cl

Vespasian
Gdns

4

Saxonwood
School for the
Handicapped

Kingsclere
Rd

Roman Rd

Augustus Dr

1

2

Waterloo Av

Tiberius
Cl

Dunsford Crs

Rose Hodson
Pl

Wellington

A339(T)

Terrace

Napole
Dr

5

Hazelw

PO

Arundel
Gdns

Beech

Way

Willow
Wy

Sycamore Wy

Astmoor

Oaklands Way

Firs

Elmwood

Way

Cedar Way

Laburnum Way

Hawthorn

Sycal

Restormel
Cl

Carlisle
Cl

Thorn Way

Warwick Rd

Lilac Way

E F 37 G H

Kenilworth
Rd

Fort Hill
School

Pendennis Cl

Tintagel
Cl

Pendennis
Cl

Warwick
Rd

Warwick
Rd

Willough

man Road

Winklebury

Warwick Rd

Willo

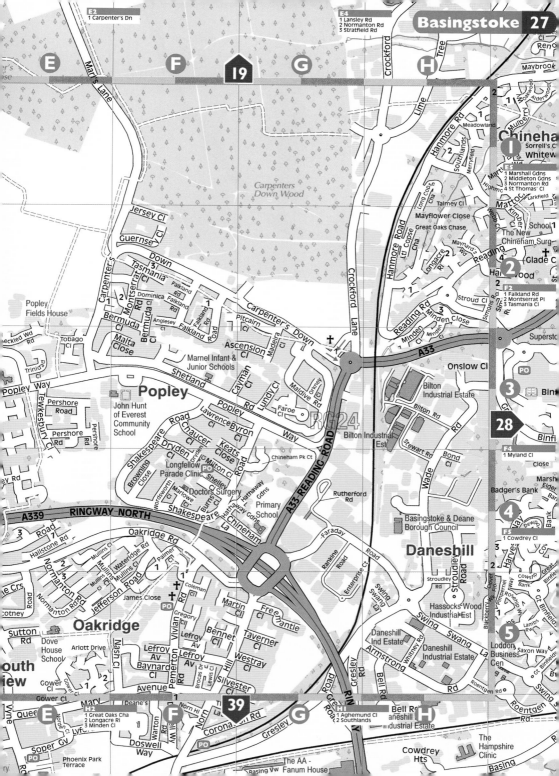

Moulshay Farm

E F **21** G H

I

2

Blackland's Farm

Hale Farm

Deanlands
Farm

3

Newnham Lane

Newnham Lane

Poors Farm

Poors Farm Road

Pot Lane

Lane

Gold's Farm

4

Water

End Lane

5

London Road

A30

Ashmoor Lane

Hod... Fm

E F **41** G H

Andwell Lane

Water E

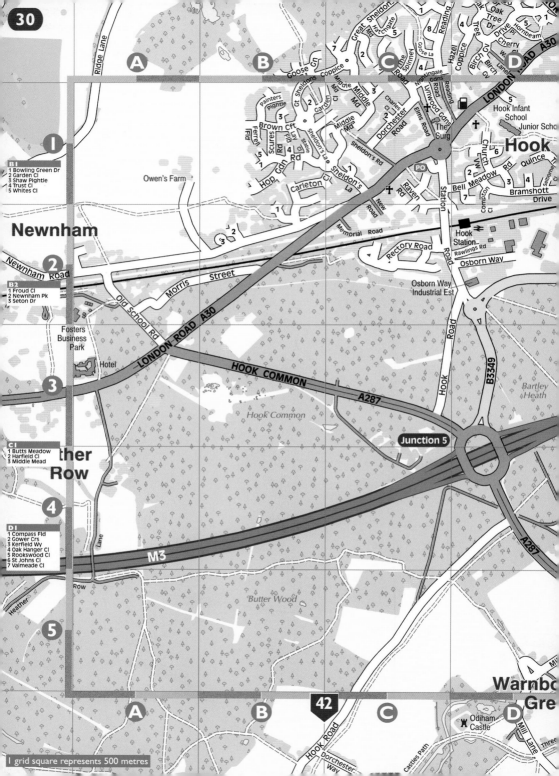

Hotel

E **F** **G** **H**

Holt Lane

5
2
Four Acre
Coppice
6
Whitewater
Rise
1
Way

2

Pantile
Dr
Bow
Fld
Bow
Field
3
Smallfield
Dr

GRIFFIN WAY SOUTH

Bow
Fld

Holt

Wild
Herons
5
Driftway
Rd

Vetch

Wy

Bartley Way

Holt Lane

Bartley Wood
Business Park

Scotland Farm

I

E1
1 Farm Ground Cl
2 Four Acre Copp
3 Hunts Cl
4 Ravens Cft
5 Wild Herons

Totters La

2

Potbridge

3

EIGHAM

Potbridge Road

B3016

M3

Poland
Mill

Poland Lane

Whitehall

4

Derby
Fields

Poland Farm

Lodge Farm

5

HOOK ROAD

Mill
Lane

LONDON ROAD

A287

gh

E **F** **43** **G** **H**

Basingstoke Canal

ICE ROAD

2

King
Wy

Clevedge

North

Oak

A   B   23   C   D

1
A3
1 Winchfield Ct

Palelane Farm

Elvetham Road

READING ROAD N

Glendale Pk

Broomrigg Road

A3

2
C3
1 Belvedere Cl

Pale Lane

Fitzroy Road

Perry Dr

3
D3
1 Monks Rl

The Oaks

Dukes

Mead

Priory Cl

Close

hurst

Calthorpe Park School

Woodcote Gn

Tavistock Rd

4
D4
1 Broadacres
2 Chantreys
3 Fieldway
4 Shaldon Wy
5 The Spinney
6 Tavistock Rd

Hart Sports Centre

Tavistock Rd

Road

Tavistock County Infant School

Junior School

New Barn

5

Hitches Lane

Larner Cl

Netherhouse

Swan Way

Hawk Gv

Dogmersfield C of E Primary School

A   **Dogmer**   B   44   C   D

D5
1 Leawood Rd
2 Netherhouse Mr
3 New Barn Cl

Pilcot

Road

Crookham Village

1 grid square represents 500 metres

A   B   C   D

1

2

Frith
Wood

Great
Deane Wood

3

Ashe
Warren Ho

Li

4

Deane Do

Harrow Way

5

Wayfarer's Walk

A   B   C   D

White

1 grid square represents 500 metres

E F G H

Shear
Down Farm

I

Malshangar House

2

Summer Down Lane

3

36 RG2

Summer Down Farm

N

4

Dell

Wood

Wayfarer's Walk

Ivy Down Lane

Malshanger Lane

H

Tollgate

Pack Lane

Turnpike Way

Boon Way

Wither Rise

Lightsfield

Clarken Green

B3400

Glamis

Highland

Barra

Arran Cl

Kintyre Cl

Braemar Dr

Park Cl

Glebe

Oakley Lane

Cad

Tanner's Cl

Church
Oakley

Mull Cl

Oban Cl

Caithness Cl

Lomond Close

Croft Rd

Avon Cl

7

2

Meon

Rd

E F 52 Road G H

OVER ROAD

County
Infant
School

PO

Lutton
Gdns

The Vale

Kennet

Stout Road

Oakley C of E
Junior School

Oakley Lane

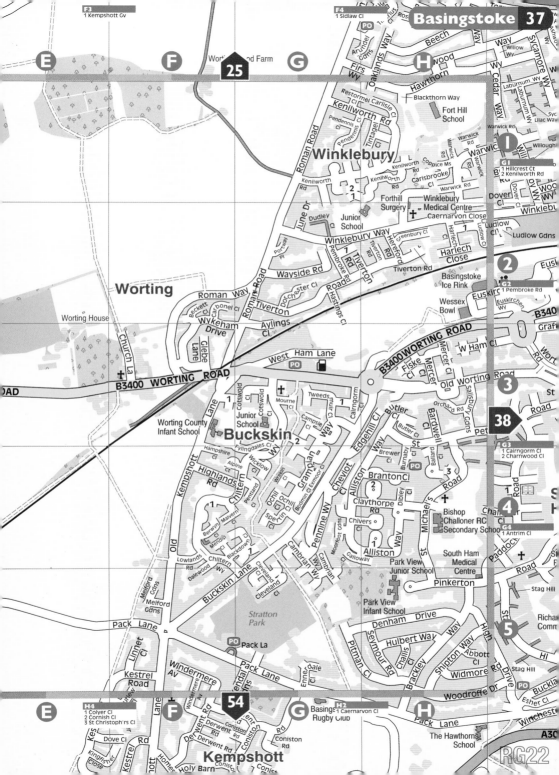

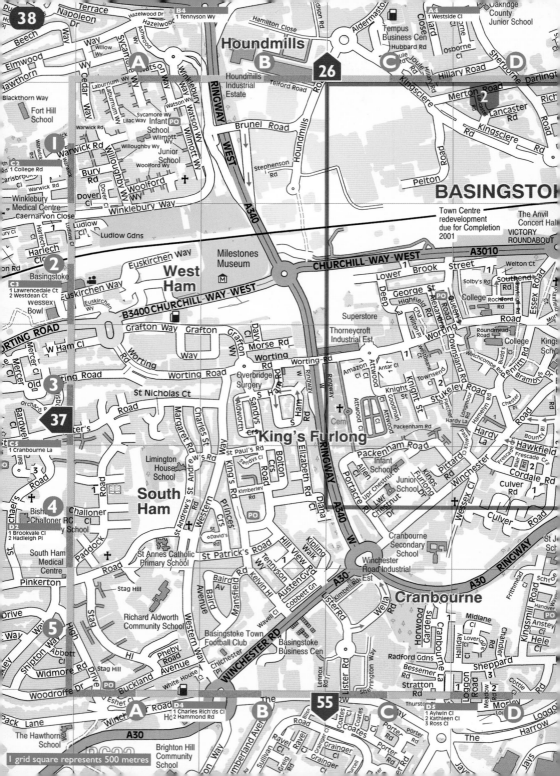

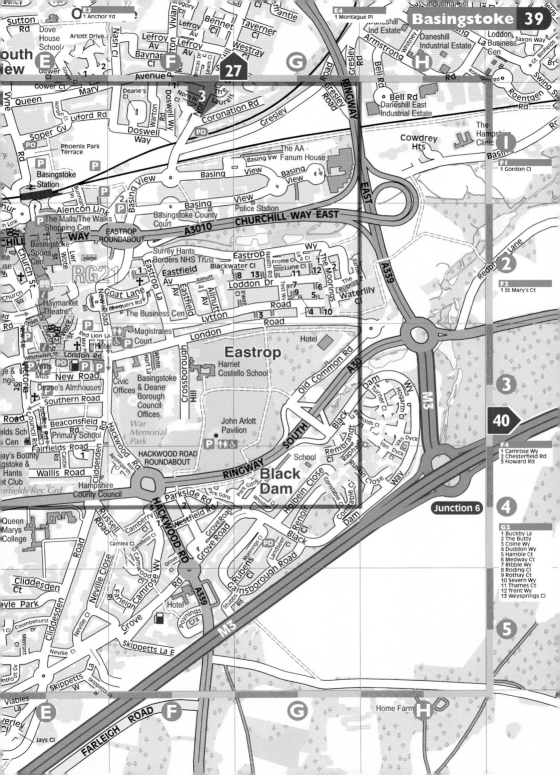

Old Basing

1 grid square represents 500 metres

E

F

29

G

H

Water E

London Road

A30

End

Lane

Lane

Ashmoor

Lane

Andwell

I

Hodd's Fm

London
Rd

Priory Farm

Andwell

or Dr

Greywell Road

M3

Greywell Road

Up Na

2

Greywell Road

tch

Greywell Road

Frog Lane

3

Tunworth

Road

Mapledurwell

4

Down

Lane

Gray's Farm

Hungry
Lodge

5

E

Tunworth Road

F

G

Down

Lane

H

Castles

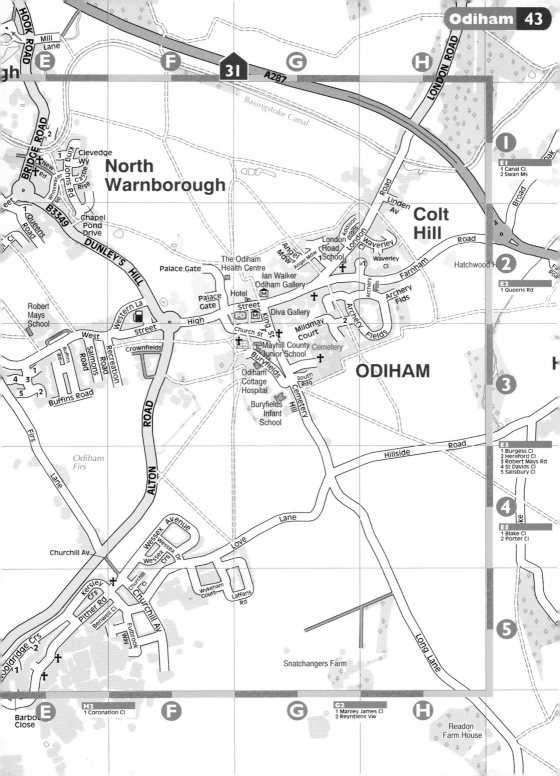

HOOK ROAD

Mill Lane

E

F

31 A287

G

H

LONDON ROAD

Basingstoke Canal

BRIDGE ROAD

New Rd
King Johns Rd
Whitewater
Castle Rise
Clevedge Wy

North Warnborough

Chapel Pond Drive

B3349

DUNLEY'S HILL

Queens Road

Robert Mays School

Western La

West Salmons Road

Recreation Road

Buffins Rd

Crownfields

Buffins Road

ALTON ROAD

Odiham Firs

Palace Gate

The Odiham Health Centre

Ian Walker Odiham Gallery

Palace Gate

Hotel

Street

High Street

King St

PO

Diva Gallery

Church St

Mildmay Court

Mayhill County Junior School

Buryfields

Odiham Cottage Hospital

Buryfields Infant School

Cemetery Hill

South Rdg

Cemetery

Angel Mdw

Angel Mdw

London Road School

Addison Gdns

London Road

Waverley Av

Waverley Cl

Linden Av

Archery Gdns

Archery Flds

Archery Fields

Farnham Road

Colt Hill

Hatchwood H

ODIHAM

Hillside Road

Love Lane

Wessex Avenue

Wessex Dr
Wessex Crs
Churchill Cl

Wykeham Court

Laffans Rd

Churchill Av

Kersley Crs

Pither Rd

Benwell Cl

Fullbrook Way

Churchill Av

Souldridge Crs

Barbou Close

Long Lane

Snatchangers Farm

Readon Farm House

E

F

G

H

I

E1
1 Canal Cl
2 Swan Ms

2

E2
1 Queens Rd

3

E3
1 Burgess Cl
2 Hereford Cl
3 Robert Mays Rd
4 St Davids Cl
5 Salisbury Cl

4

E5
1 Blake Cl
2 Porter Cl

5

Broad

46

A   B   Hogdigging Copse   C   D

Jamaica Farm

1

Harrow

2

Dirty Corner   Bloswood Lane

New
Barn Farm

3

Harroway

Cowdown
Copse

4

5

The
Mansion

A   B   C   D

Hürstbourne
Park

1 grid square represents 500 metres

RG28

Wooldings Farm

I

2

3

48

4

5

Barrow

A34(T)

Newbury Hill

Harroway

Down Farm

Newbury Road

Harroway

Berehill Farm

Whitchurch
Station

Greenwoods

Station Rd

Fairfield

Newbury District Council

Bere Hill

Bere Hill Cl

Dances Lane

Kingsley Pk

Evingar Industrial Est

Evingar Road

Evingar Gdns

Skylark Rise

Witan Ct

Caesar's Way

Canwing Rise

Meadow Vw

Bloswood Drive

Bloswood Lane

Bices Cl

Ker Ct

Firs Way

Oakland Rd

Kings Wk

Kings Wk

Lynch Hill

Lynch Hill Park

London Road

WHITCHURCH

Lwr Evingar Road

Ardglen

Newbury St

Bellevue

Newbury Road

Lynch Hill

Manor Farm

Bell Street

Great

The Lynch

Town Mill Lane

The Green

The Gables

Whitchurch
Medical Centre

CHURCH STREET

LONDON ST

PH

PO

Lynch Hill

Wells's Lane

Mill

Winchester Street

Test Road

Whitchurch C of E
Primary School

McFauld Way

Daniel Rd

Alliston Wy

Broadway

Bandon Cl

Neuvic Wy

Wheeler Cl

Brooks

Cemetery

River Test

E   F   G   H

E F G H

Hill
Meadow

Elm Rd
Beech
Cl
Copse Road

Foxdown

I

Overton
Surgery

Waltham
Rd

Riverside

Court Farm

Primary
School

Lordsfield Gdns

Court Drove

Church
Road

Overton
Gallery

Overton
Surgery

Station
Road

2

LONDON

Lynch

The Lynch

Silk Mill Lane

Glebe
Meadow

Bridge St

White Hart
Gallery

PO
1

Battens
Avenue

The Greer

Gate

The Lynch

Southington
Close

Southington La

HIGH ST

King's
Meadow

Harvey's
Fld

Red Lion Lane

Pointz
Rd

Woodlands

Lion
Cl

The Orchard

Winchester Street

Two
Paper

Mede
Close
Pound Rd

Nigh
R

Southington

B3400

Vinns
Lane

Dellands Lane

Oak Close

Ketcher's Fld

Dellands

Crawts Road

Greyhound
La

Alexander Road

Sapley Lane

3

50

ROTTEN HILL

Charledown
Cl

Close

Charledown
Road

Poultons Road

Poultons

Pond Close

4

ROTTEN HILL

toke

Turrill Hill Farm

5

Sapl
Farm

E F G H

E F **34** G H

ANDOVER ROAD

I

Deane

✝

ANDOVER ROAD PH

2

B3400

Cheesedown Farm

Ashe
Park

3

52

4

5

E F G H

Steventon

Wayfarer's Walk

Church Oakley

35

Rectory Road

Andover Road

County Infant School

Oakley C of E Junior School

OAKLEY

Arran Cl

Brae Dr

Mull Cl

Oba

Caithness Cl

Lomond Cl

Station

Oakley Hill

Beech Tree Cl

Ash

Bull's Bushes Copse

Wayfarer's Walk

Wayfarer's Walk

Bul

Dea Hea Cop

51

A   B   C   D

1

2

3

4

5

A   B   C   D

1 grid square represents 500 metres

East Oakley 36

Battledown Farm

G

H

E

F

E1
1 Blackwater Cl
2 Hamble Cl
3 Medina Gdns

Osprey Rd

Pheasant Close
Woodpecker Close
Blackbird Cl
Gannet Close
Sandpiper Wy
Teal Crs
Auklet Cl
Mallard Close
Gracemere
Fulmar
Woodmer Croft
Bunt. Close
Yellowhan

54

4

Breach Farm

Pardown

Pardown

South Wood

Club House

Golf Course

WINCHESTER ROAD

A3

2

3

5

Medway Av
Medway
Springfield
St John's Road
Oakley
Meon Road
Itchen Cl
Tamar Way
Dever Way
Avon Way
Anton
Frome Close
Matthews Way
Kennet Rd
Lyde Close
Hoopers Way
Link Way
The Drive
Hazel Cl
Oak Cl
St John's Piece
Goddards Firs
St John's Road
Hill
Kings Orchard
Yew Tree
Water Ridges
Sunny Mead
Fairview Meadow
The Surgery
Sainfoin Lane
Wayf Walk
Tisbury
Stour Road
Tefton Road
Severn Gdns

E

F

G

H

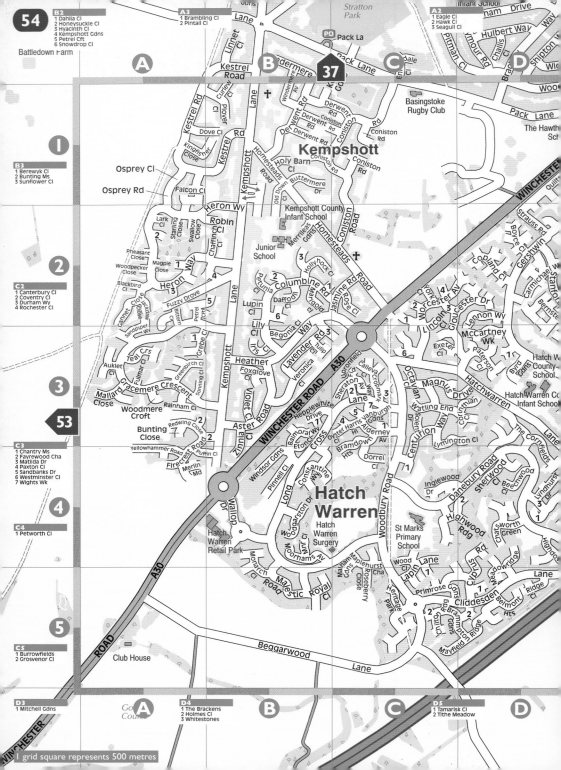

B3349

NEW ODIHAM ROAD

B4
1 Buckingham Cl
2 Sandringham Cl
3 Windsor Cl

Southwood Farm

Amery Wood

White

Curlews

Burning

Divers Cl
Eagle Cl

Finches

Gilbert Cl

Yellowhammers
Cl

Grebe Close

Fantails

Grebe

B5
1 Elmwood Cl

Rookswood

Wooteys

Partridge
Green
Mallards
Widgeons

Chestnut

Linnets
Way

1

2
C2
1 Southview Ri

Hawthorns

Southview Rd
Cherryway

Idler

Old Odiham Road

Walnut

Alton
College

Cemetery

Oakdene
PO
Lime Av

Lime Cl

Southview
Rise

Vyne
Cl

Avenue

Junior
Cemetery

3

Brick

Kiln

Lane

Kellynch

Beavers

Amery Hill
Secondary
Sch

Spitalfiel

Musgrove
Gdns

Greenfields

Netherfield Close

St Lawrence
C of E
(Controlled)
Primary Sch

Steeple

Amery Hi

St Lawrenc

Chauntsingers

Northanger

Thorpe Gdns

Tilney Cl

Bennet Cl

Brick

Kiln

Lane

Willoughby

Wentworth
Gdns

Brandon

Bingley Cl

Oliver Ri

Church St

St Cur

Allen
Gallery

Mus

Tanhouse
La

Vic

C4
1 The Cooperage
2 Duchess Cl

ALTON

Fielders

Amery
St

Market St

Street

Drayman's

A339

Will
Hall Farm

B3349

Basingstoke
Road

Lenten Street

Hill

Market Sq

High

Lower Tu

4

D2
1 Hillside Cl
2 Maple Cl
3 Vyne Cl

Balmoral
Cl

Osborne
Cl

Princess
Drive

3 7 2

2

Langham
Rd

Kingsland
Rd

Ackender Rd

Westbrooke Rd

PO

Matings

St

BASINGSTOKE ROAD

Highridge

Will
Hall
Close

Highridge

Dukes
Cl
Knights Wy

Kings

Cavalier
Wy

Whitedown La

Queens Road

Road

Rack Cl

Newtown

Old Acre Rd

Grove

Mount Pleasant Rd

St

Wyards Farm

5

Whitedown
Lane

A339

Whitedown
Downs La

Bolle Rd

The Butts
County
Primary Sch

Borovere
Gdns

Borovere

Albert
Rd

Bow
St

Tower
St

Upper

Vicarage
Rd

Goodwood

Kempton
Cl

Goodwood

Epso

Dashwood

Beechwood Road

Wickham

WHITEDOWN LANE

Whitedown Special
Sch

Butts
MS

Borovere Lane

Berehurst

Font
well
Cl

JG

Windsor

PK

Butts Road

The Butts

Lincoln
Cl

Archery

Green

D4
1 Cross & Pillory La

Commu
Hospital

Chawton Park Road

SELBORNE

ter Road

D5
1 Calender Cl
2 Churchill Cl
3 Plumpton Wy

1 grid square represents 500 metres

Alton	58 C4	Crookham Village	44 C1
Andover	57 E3	Cufaude	19 H2
Andwell	41 H2	Daneshill	27 H4
Ashe	50 D2	Deane	51 F1
Basingstoke	2 C2	Dogmersfield	44 A1
Baughurst	4 A4	East Oakley	36 B5
Black Dam	3 J7	Eastrop	3 J5
Bramley	15 H2	Ecchinswell	8 B3
Bramley Corner	15 E3	Elvetham	23 F4
Brighton Hill	55 E2	Fleet	33 G3
Browninghill Green	12 C3	Freefolk	48 A4
Buckskin	37 F3	Greywell	42 A2
The Butts	58 C5	Hartfordbridge	22 D1
Charlton	56 C1	Hartley Wintney	22 C3
Charter Alley	17 E1	Hatch	40 D2
Chineham	28 A1	Hatch Warren	54 B4
Church Crookham	45 F2	Heath End	4 C2
Church End	20 D3	Holt	31 F1
Church Oakley	35 F5	Hook	30 D1
Clarken Green	35 E5	Houndmills	26 B5
Cliddesden	55 G3	Kempshott	54 B1
Colt Hill	43 H2	Kingsclere	9 F5
Court Corner	13 G3	King's Furlong	2 A6
Cranbourne	38 C5	Latchmere Green	14 D1

Laverstoke	48 D5	Salters Heath	18 A1
Little London	14 A3	Sherborne St John	26 A1
Lynch	49 F2	Sherfield on Loddon	21 F1
Lynch Hill	47 G5	Silchester	6 C3
Mapledurwell	41 F4	South Ham	38 A4
Monk Sherborne	17 G3	Southington	49 G3
Newfound	36 A4	South View	27 E5
Newtown	58 B5	Stony Heath	12 A5
North Warnborough	43 E1	Tadley	5 F4
Oakley	52 D1	Three Ashes	7 E4
Oakridge	27 E5	Towns End	11 F4
Odiham	43 G3	Upper Wootton	24 B2
Old Basing	40 B1	Warnborough Green	42 D1
Overton	50 A3	West Ham	38 A2
Pamber End	13 G5	West Heath	12 D5
Pamber Green	13 H2	Whitchurch	47 F5
Pamber Heath	5 G1	Whitehall	31 H4
Pardown	53 E4	Wildmoor	21 F4
Popley	27 E3	Wilsom	59 E3
Pound Green	12 A3	Winklebury	37 G1
Pyott's Hill	28 B3	Wolverton	11 E5
Quidhampton	50 A1	Wolverton Common	11 F3
Ramsdell	16 D2	Wootton St Lawrence	24 C5
Rotten Green	23 H4	Worting	37 F2

USING THE STREET INDEX

Street names are listed alphabetically. Each street name is followed by its postal town or area locality, the Postcode District, the page number, and the reference to the square in which the name is found.

Example: **Abbottswood Cl** *TADY* RG26............... **5 E4** 🔲

Some entries are followed by a number in a blue box. This number indicates the location of the street within the referenced grid square. The full street name is listed at the side of the map page.

GENERAL ABBREVIATIONS

ACC	ACCESS	EMB	EMBANKMENT	LK	LOCK	RDG	RIDGE
ALY	ALLEY	EMBY	EMBASSY	LKS	LAKES	REP	REPUBLIC
AP	APPROACH	ESP	ESPLANADE	LNDG	LANDING	RES	RESERVOIR
AR	ARCADE	EST	ESTATE	LTL	LITTLE	RFC	RUGBY FOOTBALL CLUB
ASS	ASSOCIATION	EX	EXCHANGE	LWR	LOWER	RI	RISE
AV	AVENUE	EXPY	EXPRESSWAY	MAG	MAGISTRATE	RP	RAMP
BCH	BEACH	EXT	EXTENSION	MAN	MANSIONS	RW	ROW
BLDS	BUILDINGS	F/O	FLYOVER	MD	MEAD	S	SOUTH
BND	BEND	FC	FOOTBALL CLUB	MDW	MEADOWS	SCH	SCHOOL
BNK	BANK	FK	FORK	MEM	MEMORIAL	SE	SOUTH EAST
BR	BRIDGE	FLD	FIELD	MKT	MARKET	SER	SERVICE AREA
BRK	BROOK	FLDS	FIELDS	MKTS	MARKETS	SH	SHORE
BTM	BOTTOM	FLS	FALLS	ML	MALL	SHOP	SHOPPING
BUS	BUSINESS	FLS	FLATS	ML	MILL	SKWY	SKYWAY
BVD	BOULEVARD	FM	FARM	MNR	MANOR	SMT	SUMMIT
BY	BYPASS	FT	FORT	MS	MEWS	SOC	SOCIETY
CATH	CATHEDRAL	FWY	FREEWAY	MSN	MISSION	SP	SPUR
CEM	CEMETERY	FY	FERRY	MT	MOUNT	SPR	SPRING
CEN	CENTRE	GA	GATE	MTN	MOUNTAIN	SQ	SQUARE
CFT	CROFT	GAL	GALLERY	MTS	MOUNTAINS	ST	STREET
CH	CHURCH	GDN	GARDEN	MUS	MUSEUM	STN	STATION
CHA	CHASE	GDNS	GARDENS	MWY	MOTORWAY	STR	STREAM
CHYD	CHURCHYARD	GLD	GLADE	N	NORTH	STRD	STRAND
CIR	CIRCLE	GLN	GLEN	NE	NORTH EAST	SW	SOUTH WEST
CIRC	CIRCUS	GN	GREEN	NW	NORTH WEST	TDG	TRADING
CL	CLOSE	GND	GROUND	O/P	OVERPASS	TER	TERRACE
CLFS	CLIFFS	GRA	GRANGE	OFF	OFFICE	THWY	THROUGHWAY
CMP	CAMP	GRG	GARAGE	ORCH	ORCHARD	TNL	TUNNEL
CNR	CORNER	GT	GREAT	OV	OVAL	TOLL	TOLLWAY
CO	COUNTY	GTWY	GATEWAY	PAL	PALACE	TPK	TURNPIKE
COLL	COLLEGE	GV	GROVE	PAS	PASSAGE	TR	TRACK
COM	COMMON	HGR	HIGHER	PAV	PAVILION	TRL	TRAIL
COMM	COMMISSION	HL	HILL	PDE	PARADE	TWR	TOWER
CON	CONVENT	HLS	HILLS	PH	PUBLIC HOUSE	U/P	UNDERPASS
COT	COTTAGE	HO	HOUSE	PK	PARK	UNI	UNIVERSITY
COTS	COTTAGES	HOL	HOLLOW	PKWY	PARKWAY	UPR	UPPER
CP	CAPE	HOSP	HOSPITAL	PL	PLACE	V	VALE
CPS	COPSE	HRB	HARBOUR	PLN	PLAIN	VA	VALLEY
CR	CREEK	HTH	HEATH	PLNS	PLAINS	VIAD	VIADUCT
CREM	CREMATORIUM	HTS	HEIGHTS	PLZ	PLAZA	VIL	VILLA
CRS	CRESCENT	HVN	HAVEN	POL	POLICE STATION	VIS	VISTA
CSWY	CAUSEWAY	HWY	HIGHWAY	PR	PRINCE	VLG	VILLAGE
CT	COURT	IMP	IMPERIAL	PREC	PRECINCT	VLS	VILLAS
CTRL	CENTRAL	IN	INLET	PREP	PREPARATORY	VW	VIEW
CTS	COURTS	IND EST	INDUSTRIAL ESTATE	PRIM	PRIMARY	W	WEST
CTYD	COURTYARD	INF	INFIRMARY	PROM	PROMENADE	WD	WOOD
CUTT	CUTTINGS	INFO	INFORMATION	PRS	PRINCESS	WHF	WHARF
CV	COVE	INT	INTERCHANGE	PRT	PORT	WK	WALK
CYN	CANYON	IS	ISLAND	PT	POINT	WKS	WALKS
DEPT	DEPARTMENT	JCT	JUNCTION	PTH	PATH	WLS	WELLS
DL	DALE	JTY	JETTY	PZ	PIAZZA	WY	WAY
DM	DAM	KG	KING	QD	QUADRANT	YD	YARD
DR	DRIVE	KNL	KNOLL	QU	QUEEN	YHA	YOUTH HOSTEL
DRO	DROVE	L	LAKE	QY	QUAY		
DRY	DRIVEWAY	LA	LANE	R	RIVER		
DWGS	DWELLINGS	LDG	LODGE	RBT	ROUNDABOUT		
E	EAST	LGT	LIGHT	RD	ROAD		

POSTCODE TOWNS AND AREA ABBREVIATIONS

ALTN..Alton
AND..Andover
BLKW..................................Blackwater
BSTK...............................Basingstoke
CHIN................................Chineham
DEAN......................Deane/Oakley
FARN........................Farnborough
FLET.......................................Fleet
HTWY...................Hartley Wintney
KEMP..............................Kempshott
KSCL................Kingsclere/Rural Newbury
ODIM..Odiham
OVTN.............Overton/Rural Basingstoke
RAND.............................Rural Andover
RFNM.............................Rural Farnham
STHA...............................Thatcham south
TADY......................................Tadley
THLE...............Theale/Rural Reading
WHCH.............................Whitchurch

Abb - Bun

A

Abbey Rd *CHIN* RG24 .... 26 D3
Abbots Cl *FLET* GU13 .... 33 G3
Abbott Cl *KEMP* RG22 .... 37 H5
Abbottswood Cl *TADY* RG26 ...... 5 E4 ⬛
Accentors Cl *ALTN* GU34 .... 58 D1
Achilles Cl *CHIN* RG24 .... 20 A5
Ackender Rd *ALTN* GU34 .... 58 C4
Acre Pth *AND* SP10 .... 57 F3
Adam Cl *TADY* RG26 .... 4 B2
Adams Dr *FLET* GU13 .... 33 H3
Adams Wy *ALTN* GU34 .... 59 E3
Addison Gdns *ODIM* RG29 ...... 43 G2
Adelaide Rd *AND* SP10 .... 57 F3
Admirals Wy *AND* SP10 .... 57 H3
Adrian Cl *HTWY* RG27 .... 22 B4
Aghemund Cl *CHIN* RG24 ...... 27 H1 ⬛
Ajax Cl *CHIN* RG24 .... 20 A5
Alanbrooke Cl *HTWY* RG27 ...... 22 A3
Albany Cl *FLET* GU13 .... 33 H4
Albany Rd *AND* SP10 .... 56 C3
  FLET GU13 .... 33 G4
Albert Rd *ALTN* GU34 .... 58 C5
Albert St *FLET* GU13 .... 33 F3
Alder Cl *ALTN* GU34 .... 58 C2
Aldermaston Rd *TADY* RG26 ...... 4 D1
  TADY RG26 .... 13 G1
Aldermaston Rd South
  BSTK RG21 .... 26 C5
Alderney Av *KEMP* RG22 ...... 54 C3
Aldershot Rd *FLET* GU13 ...... 45 F5
Alderwood *CHIN* RG24 .... 28 A1
Aldworth Crs *KEMP* RG22 ...... 38 B3
Alencon Link *BSTK* RG21 .... 2 D3
Alexander Rd *OVTN* RG25 ...... 49 H3
Alexandra Rd *ALTN* GU34 ...... 58 D2
  AND SP10 .... 56 D3
  BSTK RG21 .... 2 B4
Allen Cl *ALTN* GU34 .... 59 E2
  BSTK RG21 .... 2 A7
Alliston Wy *KEMP* RG22 .... 37 H4
Allnutt Av *BSTK* RG21 .... 3 H4
Almond Cl *CHIN* RG24 .... 40 B1
Almswood Rd *TADY* RG26 .... 4 D1
The Aloes *FLET* GU13 .... 33 H4
Alpine Cl *KEMP* RG22 .... 37 F4
Alton Rd *ODIM* RG29 .... 43 F4
Amazon Cl *BSTK* RG21 .... 2 A5
Amber Gdns *AND* SP10 .... 56 B3
Ambrose Rd *TADY* RG26 .... 5 E3
Amery Hl *ALTN* GU34 .... 58 D3
Amery St *ALTN* GU34 .... 58 D4
Amport Cl *CHIN* RG24 .... 28 B4 ⬛
Anchor Rd *KSCL* RG20 .... 9 G4
Anchor Yd *BSTK* RG21 .... 3 F5
Andover Rd *DEAN* RG23 ...... 52 A1
  OVTN RG25 .... 51 F2
Andrews Cl *FLET* GU13 .... 45 G1
Andwell La *HTWY* RG27 .... 41 H1
Angel Mdw *ODIM* RG29 .... 43 G2
Anglesey Cl *CHIN* RG24 .... 27 F2
Annes Wy *FLET* GU13 .... 45 H1
Annettes Cft *FLET* GU13 ...... 45 E3 ⬛
Anstey Cl *BSTK* RG21 .... 38 D5
Anstey Mill Cl *ALTN* GU34 ...... 59 F2
Anstey Mill La *ALTN* GU34 ...... 59 F2
Anstey Rd *ALTN* GU34 .... 59 E3
Antar Cl *BSTK* RG21 .... 2 A5
Anton Cl *DEAN* RG23 .... 53 E1
Anton Mill Rd *AND* SP10 ...... 56 D5
Anton Rd *AND* SP10 .... 57 E5
Antrim Cl *KEMP* RG22 ...... 37 G4 ⬛
Applegarth Cl *BSTK* RG21 .... 3 C7
Appletree Cl *DEAN* RG23 ...... 53 E2
Apple Tree Gv *AND* SP10 ...... 56 B3
Apple Wy *CHIN* RG24 .... 40 C2
Archery Flds *ODIM* RG29 ...... 43 H2
Archery Ri *ALTN* GU34 .... 58 C5
Ardglen Rd *WHCH* RG28 ...... 47 E5
Arlott Dr *BSTK* RG21 .... 27 E5
Armstrong Rd *CHIN* RG24 ...... 27 H5
Arne Cl *KEMP* RG22 ...... 55 E3 ⬛
Arran Cl *DEAN* RG23 .... 35 H5
Artists Wy *AND* SP10 .... 56 D2
Arundel Cl *FLET* GU13 .... 33 H4

Arundel Gdns *DEAN* RG23 ...... 25 G5
Arwood Av *TADY* RG26 .... 5 G2 ⬛
Ascension Cl *CHIN* RG24 ...... 27 F3
Ascot Cl *ALTN* GU34 .... 59 E5
Ashdell Rd *ALTN* GU34 .... 59 E4
Ashfield *CHIN* RG24 .... 28 A1
Ashfield Rd *AND* SP10 .... 56 B3
Ash Gv *CHIN* RG24 .... 40 D1
  KSCL RG20 .... 9 G4
Ash La *TADY* RG26 .... 4 B2
  TADY RG26 .... 15 E1
Ashlawn Gdns *AND* SP10 ...... 57 F5
Ashmoor La *CHIN* RG24 .... 41 F1
Ash Tree Cl *DEAN* RG23 ...... 52 D2
Ash Tree Rd *AND* SP10 .... 56 A3
Ashurst Cl *TADY* RG26 .... 4 D3 ⬛
Ashwood Wy *DEAN* RG23 ...... 26 A5
Aster Rd *KEMP* RG22 .... 54 B3
Atbara Rd *FLET* GU13 .... 45 G3
Attenborough Cl *FARN* GU14 .... 33 H1
Attlee Gdns *FLET* GU13 .... 45 F3
Attwood Cl *BSTK* RG21 .... 2 A5
Augustus Dr *DEAN* RG23 ...... 25 H5
Auklet Cl *KEMP* RG22 .... 54 A3
Austen Gv *KEMP* RG22 .... 38 B5
Avenue Cl *AND* SP10 .... 56 C3
Avenue Rd *FLET* GU13 .... 33 F2
The Avenue *AND* SP10.............. 56 C3
  FLET GU13 .... 33 E3
Avon Cl *AND* SP10 .... 57 G1 ⬛
Avondale Rd *FLET* GU13 ...... 33 G2
Avon Rd *DEAN* RG23 .... 53 E1
Award Rd *FLET* GU13 .... 45 F2
Ayesgarth *FLET* GU13 .... 45 H2
Aylings Cl *DEAN* RG23 .... 37 G3
Aylwin Cl *BSTK* RG21 ...... 38 D5 ⬛
Azalea Gdns *FLET* GU13 ...... 45 H2

B

Bach Cl *KEMP* RG22 .... 55 E3
Badger's Bank *CHIN* RG24 ...... 28 A4
Badgers Cl *FLET* GU13 .... 33 F4
Baird Av *KEMP* RG22 .... 38 B5
Ballard Cl *KEMP* RG22 .... 37 H4
Balmoral Cl *ALTN* GU34 ...... 58 B4
Balmoral Rd *AND* SP10 .... 57 E3
Balmoral Wy *KEMP* RG22 ...... 54 B3
Barbara Cl *FLET* GU13 .... 45 H1
Barbel Av *BSTK* RG21 .... 3 K3
Barberry Cl *FLET* GU13 .... 45 G1
Barcelona Cl *AND* SP10 ...... 57 F2 ⬛
Bardwell Cl *KEMP* RG22 ...... 37 H5
Barlows Rd *TADY* RG26 .... 5 F2
Barnfield Ri *AND* SP10............ 56 C5
Barn La *DEAN* RG23 .... 52 D2
Barn Meadow Cl *FLET* GU13...... 45 F4
Barra Cl *DEAN* RG23 .... 35 H5
Barron Pl *CHIN* RG24 .... 25 C4
Barry Wy *KEMP* RG22 .... 55 E3
Bartley Wy *HTWY* RG27 ...... 31 E2
Bartok Cl *KEMP* RG22 .... 55 F1
Bartons La *CHIN* RG24 .... 28 B4
Basingbourne Cl *FLET* GU13...... 45 G1
Basingbourne Rd *FLET* GU13 .... 45 F1
Basing Rd *CHIN* RG24 .... 40 A1
Basingstoke Rd *ALTN* GU34 ...... 58 C4
  KSCL RG20 .... 9 H4
  TADY RG26 .... 16 D4
Basing Vw *BSTK* RG21 .... 3 H2
Batchelor Dr *CHIN* RG24 ...... 40 D2
Batchelors Barn Rd *AND* SP10.... 57 G3
Battens Av *OVTN* RG25 ...... 50 A2
Baughurst Rd *TADY* RG26 .... 4 B3
Baverstocks *ALTN* GU34 ...... 59 E1
Baynard Cl *BSTK* RG21 .... 27 F5
Beach's Crs *TADY* RG26 ...... 14 B3
Beacon Hill Rd *FLET* GU13 ...... 45 H3
Beaconsfield Rd *BSTK* RG21 .... 3 F4
Beale's Cl *AND* SP10.............. 57 F3
Beal's Pightle *TADY* RG26 ...... 17 E2
Bear Hl *KSCL* RG20 .... 9 F5
Bearwood *FLET* GU13 .... 33 G3
Beaufort Cl *BSTK* RG21 .... 3 G5
Beaulieu Ct *AND* SP10 ...... 57 G1 ⬛
Beaumaris Cl *AND* SP10 ...... 56 C5

Beaurepaire Cl *TADY* RG26 ...... 15 G3
Beavers Cl *ALTN* GU34 .... 58 C3
  TADY RG26 .... 4 C2
Beckett Cl *DEAN* RG23 .... 37 F2
Beckett Rd *AND* SP10 .... 56 C3
Beddington Ct *CHIN* RG24 ...... 28 B3 ⬛
Beecham Berry *KEMP* RG22...... 55 E5
The Beeches *KEMP* RG22.......... 55 F4
Beech Ride *FLET* GU13............ 33 F5
Beech Tree Cl *DEAN* RG23 ...... 52 D2
Beech Wy *DEAN* RG23 ...... 25 H5
Beechwood Cl *FLET* GU13...... 45 E1
  KEMP RG22 .... 54 D4
Beechwood Rd *ALTN* GU34...... 58 B5
Beethoven Rd *KEMP* RG22...... 55 F2
Beggarwood La *DEAN* RG23...... 54 B5
  KEMP RG22 .... 55 E4
Begonia Cl *KEMP* RG22 ...... 54 B3
Bellevue *WHCH* RG28............ 47 F5
Belle Vue Rd *AND* SP10 ...... 57 F5
  CHIN RG24 .... 40 C1
Bell Meadow Rd *HTWY* RG27 .... 30 D1
Bell Rd *AND* SP10 .... 56 C3
  CHIN RG24 .... 27 H5
Bell St *WHCH* RG28............ 47 F5
Belmont Cl *AND* SP10 ...... 57 F5 ⬛
Belmont Hts *KEMP* RG22 ...... 54 D5
Belmont Rd *AND* SP10.............. 57 F5
Belvedere Cl *FLET* GU13 ...... 32 C3 ⬛
Belvedere Gdns *CHIN* RG24 ...... 20 B5 ⬛
Bennet Cl *ALTN* GU34 .... 58 C3
  BSTK RG21 .... 27 F5
Benwell Cl *ODIM* RG29 .... 43 E5
Bere Hl *WHCH* RG28............ 47 F4
Bere Hill Cl *WHCH* RG28............ 47 G4
Bere Hill Crs *AND* SP10............ 57 G4
Berehurst *ALTN* GU34 .... 58 C5
Berewyk Cl *KEMP* RG22 ...... 54 B3 ⬛
Berkeley Cl *FLET* GU13 ...... 33 H3 ⬛
Berkeley Dr *KEMP* RG22 ...... 55 G2
Bermuda Cl *CHIN* RG24 .... 27 F3
Bernstein Rd *KEMP* RG22 ...... 54 D2
Berrydown La *OVTN* RG25 ...... 50 B3
Berwyn Cl *KEMP* RG22 .... 37 F4
Bessemer Rd *BSTK* RG21......... 38 C5
Bexmoor *CHIN* RG24 .... 40 B1
Bexmoor Wy *CHIN* RG24 ...... 40 B1
Bicester Cl *WHCH* RG28 ...... 47 F5
Bidden Rd *ODIM* RG29 .... 42 C3
Bilbao Ct *AND* SP10 .... 57 H2
Binfields Cl *CHIN* RG24 ...... 28 A3
Bingley Cl *ALTN* GU34 .... 58 C3
Birch Av *FLET* GU13 .... 33 F3
Birches Crest *KEMP* RG22...... 55 E4
Birch Rd *TADY* RG26................ 4 B3
Birchwood *CHIN* RG24 ...... 28 A1 ⬛
Bishops Cl *FLET* GU13 .... 33 G5
  TADY RG26 .... 4 D2
Bishop's Wy *AND* SP10 ...... 56 D3
Bishopswood La *TADY* RG26 ...... 4 B2
Bishopswood Rd *TADY* RG26 ...... 4 C2
Bittern Cl *KEMP* RG22 .... 54 A2
Blackberry Wk *CHIN* RG24 ...... 28 A5 ⬛
Blackbird Pth *KEMP* RG22 ...... 54 A2
Blackbird Ct *AND* SP10 ...... 57 F1 ⬛
Black Dam Wy *BSTK* RG21 .... 3 K6
Blackdown Cl *AND* SP10 ...... 37 F4
Blackthorn Wy *DEAN* RG23...... 37 H1
Blackwater Cl *BSTK* RG21......... 3 L4
  DEAN RG23 .... 53 E1 ⬛
Blair Rd *BSTK* RG21 .... 2 B4
Blake Cl *ODIM* RG29 ...... 43 E5 ⬛
Blake's La *TADY* RG26 .... 5 E2
Blendon Dr *AND* SP10 ...... 56 B3
Blenheim Cl *ALTN* GU34 ...... 59 E4 ⬛
Blenheim Rd *CHIN* RG24 ...... 40 D2
Bliss Cl *KEMP* RG22 .... 55 F1
Bloswood Dr *WHCH* RG28 ...... 47 E5
Bloswood La *WHCH* RG28 ...... 46 C2
Blunden Cl *BSTK* RG21 ...... 55 G1
Boar's Br *TADY* RG26 ...... 14 B4
Bodmin Cl *KEMP* RG22 ...... 37 G4
Bolle Rd *ALTN* GU34 .... 58 B5
Bolton Crs *KEMP* RG22 ...... 38 B4
Bond Cl *CHIN* RG24 .... 27 H4
Boon Wy *DEAN* RG23 ...... 35 H5
Borden Gates *AND* SP10 ...... 57 E4 ⬛
Bordon Cl *TADY* RG26 .... 4 D3

Borodin Cl *KEMP* RG22 .... 55 G2
Borovere Cl *ALTN* GU34 ...... 58 C5
Borovere Gdns *ALTN* GU34 ...... 58 C5
Borovere La *ALTN* GU34 ...... 58 C5
Borsberry Cl *AND* SP10 ...... 57 F3
Bounty Ri *BSTK* RG21.............. 2 D6
Bounty Rd *BSTK* RG21.............. 2 D6
Bourne Ct *AND* SP10 ...... 57 G1 ⬛
Bourne Fld *CHIN* RG24 ...... 18 B5
The Bourne *FLET* GU13 ...... 45 G1
Bourne Rd *ALTN* GU34 .... 59 E3
Bow Dr *HTWY* RG27 .... 21 E1
Bowenhurst Gdns *FLET* GU13 ...... 45 G3
Bowenhurst Rd *FLET* GU13 ...... 45 G3
bowenhust La *NFNM* GU10 ...... 44 C4
Bow Fld *HTWY* RG27 .... 31 E1
Bow Gdns *HTWY* RG27 ...... 21 E1 ⬛
Bowling Green Dr *HTWY* RG27 . 30 B1 ⬛
Bowman Rd *CHIN* RG24 ...... 20 A5
Bowmonts Rd *TADY* RG26 .... 5 G3
Bow St *ALTN* GU34 .... 58 C5
Boyce Cl *KEMP* RG22 .... 54 D2
Bracher Cl *AND* SP10 ...... 57 F5 ⬛
Bracken Bank *CHIN* RG24 ...... 28 A4 ⬛
Brackenbury *AND* SP10 ...... 56 B2
The Brackens *KEMP* RG22 ...... 54 D4 ⬛
Brackley Av *HTWY* RG27 ...... 22 A3
Brackley Wy *KEMP* RG22 ...... 54 D1
Bracknell La *HTWY* RG27 ...... 22 B2
Bradbury Cl *WHCH* RG28 ...... 47 E5 ⬛
Braemar Dr *DEAN* RG23 ...... 35 H5
Brahms Rd *KEMP* RG22 ...... 55 F2
Bramble Wy *CHIN* RG24 ...... 40 D1
Bramblewood Pl *FLET* GU13 ...... 33 E3
Brambling Cl *KEMP* RG22 ...... 54 A3 ⬛
Bramblys Cl *BSTK* RG21.............. 2 D5
Bramblys Dr *BSTK* RG21.............. 2 C5
Bramdown Hts *KEMP* RG22 ...... 54 C4
Bramley Cl *ALTN* GU34 ...... 59 E5 ⬛
Bramley Rd *TADY* RG26 ...... 14 A5
  THLE RG7 .... 6 C2
Brampton Gdns *KEMP* RG22...... 54 C5
Bramshot Dr *FLET* GU13 ...... 33 G2
Bramshott Dr *HTWY* RG27 ...... 30 D1
Brandon Cl *ALTN* GU34 ...... 58 B3
Brandon Rd *FLET* GU13 ...... 45 E2
Branksomewood Rd *FLET* GU13 .. 33 E3
Branton Cl *KEMP* RG22 ...... 37 H4
Breach La *HTWY* RG27 ...... 22 F1
Bremen Gdns *AND* SP10 ...... 56 D1
Brewer Cl *KEMP* RG22 ...... 37 H4
Brewhouse La *HTWY* RG27 ...... 22 B3 ⬛
Briar Wy *TADY* RG26................ 5 F3
Brick Cl *CHIN* RG24 ...... 28 B4 ⬛
Brick Kiln La *ALTN* GU34 ...... 58 A3
Brick La *FLET* GU13................ 33 C2
Bridge Rd *ODIM* RG29 ...... 43 E1
Bridge St *AND* SP10 .... 57 E4
  OVTN RG25 .... 49 H2
Brighton Wy *KEMP* RG22 ...... 55 E1
Brinksway *FLET* GU13 ...... 33 G4
Broadacres *FLET* GU13 ...... 32 D4 ⬛
Broadhalfpenny La *TADY* RG26 .. 5 F2
Broadmere Rd *CHIN* RG24 ...... 28 A5
Broadoak *TADY* RG26 ...... 5 G3 ⬛
Brocas Dr *BSTK* RG21 ...... 27 F5
Brook Cl *FLET* GU13 ...... 33 G4
Brookfield Cl *CHIN* RG24 ...... 28 B1 ⬛
Brook Gn *TADY* RG26 ...... 5 G3
Brookly Gdns *FLET* GU13 ...... 33 H2
Brookvale Cl *BSTK* RG21.............. 2 C4
Broom Acres *FLET* GU13 ...... 45 F1
Broomrigg Rd *FLET* GU13 ...... 45 H1
Brown Cft *HTWY* RG27 ...... 30 B1
Browning Cl *CHIN* RG24 ...... 45 E4
Browning Rd *FLET* GU13 ...... 45 E4
Browns Cl *TADY* RG26 ...... 15 H2
Brtten Rd *KEMP* RG22 ...... 55 F2
Brunel Rd *BSTK* RG21.............. 38 B3
Bryanstone Cl *FLET* GU13 ...... 45 G1
Buckby La *BSTK* RG21 .... 3 K3
Buckfast Cl *CHIN* RG24 ...... 26 D5
Buckingham Cl *ALTN* GU34 ...... 58 B4 ⬛
Buckland Av *KEMP* RG22 ...... 55 E1
Buckskin La *KEMP* RG22 ...... 54 C4
Budd's Cl *BSTK* RG21.............. 2 A5
Buffins Rd *ODIM* RG29 ...... 43 E3
Bunnian Pl *BSTK* RG21.............. 3 F2
Bunting Cl *KEMP* RG22 ...... 54 A3 ⬛

Bunting Ms *KEMP* RG22 .... **54** B3
Buntings *ALTN* GU34 .... **58** D1
Burgess Cl *ODIM* RG29 .... **43** E3
Burgess Rd *BSTK* RG21 .... **2** D1
Burnaby Cl *KEMP* RG22 .... **37** H4
Burney Bit *TADY* RG26 .... **5** H3
Burnham Rd *TADY* RG26 .... **4** C1
Burnley Cl *TADY* RG26 .... **5** E4
Burns Av *FLET* GU13 .... **45** H1
Burns Cl *CHIN* RG24 .... **27** F4
Burrowfields *KEMP* RG22 .... **54** C5
Burton's Gdns *CHIN* RG24 .... **28** C5
Buryfields *ODIM* RG29 .... **43** E2
Bury Rd *DEAN* RG23 .... **38** A1
Bushnells Dr *KSCL* RG20 .... **9** F4
Butler Cl *KEMP* RG22 .... **37** H3
Buttermere Dr *KEMP* RG22 .... **54** B4
Butts Meadow *HTWY* RG27 .... **30** C1
Butts Ms *ALTN* GU34 .... **58** C5
The Butts *THLE* RG7 .... **6** C3
The Butty *BSTK* RG21 .... **3** K3
Byes Cl *THLE* RG7 .... **6** C4
Byfields Rd *KSCL* RG20 .... **9** F4
Byfleet Av *CHIN* RG24 .... **40** C2
Byrd Gdns *KEMP* RG22 .... **54** D3
Byron Cl *CHIN* RG24 .... **27** F3
FLET GU13 .... **33** G4

C

Cadet Wy *FLET* GU13 .... **45** H3
Cadnam Cl *DEAN* RG23 .... **36** A5
Caernarvon Cl *DEAN* RG23 .... **37** H2
Caesar's Wy *WHCH* RG28 .... **47** E4
Cairngorm Cl *KEMP* RG22 .... **37** G3
Caithness Cl *DEAN* RG23 .... **35** H5
Caker's La *ALTN* GU34 .... **59** H5
Caker Stream Rd *ALTN* GU34 .... **59** G1
Calder Cl *AND* SP10 .... **57** G1
Calender Cl *ALTN* GU34 .... **58** D5
Calleva Cl *KEMP* RG22 .... **54** C5
Calthorpe Rd *FLET* GU13 .... **33** E2
HTWY RG27 .... **33** E1
Camberry Cl *BSTK* RG21 .... **39** F4
Cambrian Wy *KEMP* RG22 .... **37** G4
Camelot Cl *AND* SP10 .... **57** E1
Camfield Cl *BSTK* RG21 .... **39** F4
Camlea Cl *BSTK* RG21 .... **39** F4
Campbell Cl *FLET* GU13 .... **33** E3
Campion Wy *HTWY* RG27 .... **22** B2
Campsie Cl *BSTK* RG21 .... **37** G3
Camrose Wy *BSTK* RG21 .... **39** F4
Camus Cl *FLET* GU13 .... **44** D2
Camwood Cl *BSTK* RG21 .... **39** F4
Canal Cl *ODIM* RG29 .... **43** E1
Candover Cl *TADY* RG26 .... **5** E4
Canon's Ct *KSCL* RG20 .... **9** F4
Canterbury Cl *KEMP* RG22 .... **54** C2
Carbonel Cl *DEAN* RG23 .... **37** F2
Carisbrooke Cl *DEAN* RG23 .... **37** H1
Carleton Cl *HTWY* RG27 .... **30** D1
Carlisle Cl *DEAN* RG23 .... **37** H1
Carlton Crs *FLET* GU13 .... **45** H1
Carmichael Wy *KEMP* RG22 .... **54** D2
Carpenter's Down *CHIN* RG24 .... **27** E2
Carrington Crs *TADY* RG26 .... **5** E3
Carter's Meadow *AND* SP10 .... **56** B1
Carthona Dr *FLET* GU13 .... **33** F5
Castle Ri *ODIM* RG29 .... **43** E1
Castle Rd *BSTK* RG21 .... **3** F7
Castle St *FLET* GU13 .... **33** F5
Castor Cl *FLET* GU13 .... **45** H2
Catkin Cl *CHIN* RG24 .... **28** A1
Cavalier Cl *CHIN* RG24 .... **40** D1
Cavalier Rd *CHIN* RG24 .... **40** D1
Cavalier Wy *ALTN* GU34 .... **58** B5
Cavel Ct *AND* SP10 .... **28** B4
Cavendish Rd *FLET* GU13 .... **45** E2
Caxton Cl *AND* SP10 .... **56** A2
Cayman Cl *CHIN* RG24 .... **27** F3
Cedar Cl *TADY* RG26 .... **5** G5
Cedar Dr *KSCL* RG20 .... **9** F4
The Cedars *FLET* GU13 .... **33** H4
Cedar Tree Cl *DEAN* RG23 .... **52** D2
Cedar Wy *DEAN* RG23 .... **26** A5
Celtic Dr *AND* SP10 .... **56** C5
Cemetery Hl *ODIM* RG29 .... **43** G3
Cemetery Rd *FLET* GU13 .... **33** E5
Centre Dr *CHIN* RG24 .... **28** A3
Centurion Wy *KEMP* RG22 .... **54** C4
Chaffinch Cl *KEMP* RG22 .... **54** C4
Chalcrafts *ALTN* GU34 .... **59** E2
Chalk V *CHIN* RG24 .... **28** A4
Challis Cl *KEMP* RG22 .... **37** H5
Challoner Cl *KEMP* RG22 .... **37** H4
Champion Wy *FLET* GU13 .... **45** G2
Chandler Rd *BSTK* RG21 .... **38** B5
Chantreys *FLET* GU13 .... **32** D4
Chantry Ms *KEMP* RG22 .... **54** C3
Chantry St *AND* SP10 .... **57** E3
Chapel Hl *BSTK* RG21 .... **2** D2

Chapel La *TADY* RG26 .... **11** E2
Chapel Pond Dr *ODIM* RG29 .... **43** E2
Chapel River Cl *KEMP* RG22 .... **56** B4
Chapter Ter *HTWY* RG27 .... **22** B3
Charldon Gn *CHIN* RG24 .... **28** B4
Charledown Cl *OVTN* RG25 .... **49** H3
Charledown Rd *OVTN* RG25 .... **49** H3
Charles Cl *HTWY* RG27 .... **30** C1
Charles Richards Cl *BSTK* RG21 .... **2** D7
Charles St *AND* SP10 .... **38** A3
Charlotte Cl *AND* SP10 .... **57** H3
Charlton Rd *AND* SP10 .... **56** C2
Charnwood Cl *AND* SP10 .... **57** F5
KEMP RG22 .... **37** G3
Chatsworth Dr *AND* SP10 .... **56** C4
Chatsworth Gn *KEMP* RG22 .... **54** D4
Chaucer Av *AND* SP10 .... **56** C2
Chaucer Cl *CHIN* RG24 .... **27** F3
Chauntsingers Rd *ALTN* GU34 .... **59** E2
Cheavley Cl *AND* SP10 .... **56** A3
Chequers Rd *BSTK* RG21 .... **3** F4
Cheriton Cl *TADY* RG26 .... **5** E4
Cherry Tree Rd *AND* SP10 .... **56** C2
Cherryway *ALTN* GU34 .... **58** C2
Chesilton Crs *FLET* GU13 .... **45** G3
Chesterfield Rd *BSTK* RG21 .... **3** H7
BSTK RG21 .... **39** F4
Chester Pl *BSTK* RG21 .... **2** C6
Chestnut Cl *ALTN* GU34 .... **58** C2
Chestnut Gv *FLET* GU13 .... **33** H2
Cheswell Gdns *FLET* GU13 .... **45** E1
Cheviot Cl *KEMP* RG22 .... **37** G4
Chichester Cl *AND* SP10 .... **56** B3
Chichester Pl *KEMP* RG22 .... **38** B5
Chiltern Cl *FLET* GU13 .... **45** H2
Chiltern Wy *KEMP* RG22 .... **37** G4
Chilton Rdg *KEMP* RG22 .... **54** C5
Chineham La *CHIN* RG24 .... **26** D2
Chineham Park Ct *CHIN* RG24 .... **27** G4
Chinnock Cl *FLET* GU13 .... **33** F5
Chivers Cl *KEMP* RG22 .... **37** H5
Chopin Rd *KEMP* RG22 .... **55** E2
Christchurch Cl *FLET* GU13 .... **45** F3
Christy Ct *TADY* RG26 .... **5** F4
Church Brook *TADY* RG26 .... **4** D5
Church Cl *AND* SP10 .... **57** F3
Church Gv *FLET* GU13 .... **33** E3
Churchill Av *ODIM* RG29 .... **43** E4
Churchill Cl *ALTN* GU34 .... **58** D5
ODIM RG29 .... **43** F5
TADY RG26 .... **5** G4
Churchill Wy *AND* SP10 .... **57** H2
BSTK RG21 .... **2** E5
Churchill Wy East *BSTK* RG21 .... **3** H3
Churchill Wy West *AND* SP10 .... **56** B1
BSTK RG21 .... **2** A4
KEMP RG22 .... **38** A2
Church Lands *TADY* RG26 .... **15** G3
Church La *CHIN* RG24 .... **40** C1
DEAN RG23 .... **37** F3
HTWY RG27 .... **22** B5
OVTN RG25 .... **55** H3
TADY RG26 .... **10** C4
THLE RG7 .... **7** F2
Church Rd *FLET* GU13 .... **33** E2
OVTN RG25 .... **49** H4
TADY RG26 .... **5** H2
TADY RG26 .... **5** E5
Church Sq *BSTK* RG21 .... **2** C5
Church St *ALTN* GU34 .... **58** D3
BSTK RG21 .... **2** E4
ODIM RG29 .... **43** F3
Church Vw *HTWY* RG27 .... **22** A4
HTWY RG27 .... **30** D1
Churn Cl *CHIN* RG24 .... **28** C5
Cibbons Rd *CHIN* RG24 .... **28** A1
Clappers Farm Rd *THLE* RG7 .... **7** H3
Clapps Gate Rd *TADY* RG26 .... **5** H2
Clarence Rd *FLET* GU13 .... **33** F4
Clarendon Av *AND* SP10 .... **56** C5
Claudius Dr *DEAN* RG23 .... **25** H5
Claythorpe Rd *KEMP* RG22 .... **37** G4
Clayton Cl *HTWY* RG27 .... **22** A4
Clemence Gdns *WHCH* RG28 .... **47** F5
Clere Gdns *CHIN* RG24 .... **28** A2
Clevedge Wy *ODIM* RG29 .... **43** E1
Cleveland Cl *KEMP* RG22 .... **37** G4
Cliddesden Ct *BSTK* RG21 .... **39** E5
Cliddesden La *KEMP* RG22 .... **54** C5
Cliddesden Rd *BSTK* RG21 .... **3** F7
Clifton Ter *BSTK* RG21 .... **3** G2
The Close *TADY* RG26 .... **17** G3
Clover Fld *CHIN* RG24 .... **28** A4
Clyde Ct *AND* SP10 .... **57** G1
Coach House Gdns *FLET* GU13 .... **33** G1
Coachways *AND* SP10 .... **57** E5
Coates Cl *KEMP* RG22 .... **55** G1
Cobbett Gn *KEMP* RG22 .... **38** B5
Colbeck Cl *FLET* GU13 .... **45** H3
Colebrook Wy *AND* SP10 .... **56** B3
Coleman Cl *BSTK* RG21 .... **27** F5
Colenzo Dr *AND* SP10 .... **57** G2
College Rd *BSTK* RG21 .... **2** B3
Colne Valley Wy *WHCH* RG28 .... **48** C5

Colne Wy *BSTK* RG21 .... **3** J4
Columbine Rd *KEMP* RG22 .... **54** B2
Colyer Cl *KEMP* RG22 .... **37** H4
Compass Fld *HTWY* RG27 .... **30** D1
Complins *ALTN* GU34 .... **59** F1
Compton Cl *FLET* GU13 .... **45** H2
HTWY RG27 .... **30** D2
Compton Rd *FLET* GU13 .... **45** H2
Conifer Cl *FLET* GU13 .... **45** F2
TADY RG26 .... **4** B2
Coniston Rd *KEMP* RG22 .... **54** C1
Coniston Wy *FLET* GU13 .... **45** E2
Connaught Rd *FLET* GU13 .... **33** G4
Constable Cl *BSTK* RG21 .... **39** G4
Constable Cl *AND* SP10 .... **57** E2
Constantine Wy *KEMP* RG22 .... **54** B4
Coombehurst Dr *BSTK* RG21 .... **39** E5
The Cooperage *ALTN* GU34 .... **58** C4
Coopers La *TADY* RG26 .... **15** H3
Copland Cl *KEMP* RG22 .... **54** D2
Coppice Cl *TADY* RG26 .... **4** A3
Coppice Ms *DEAN* RG23 .... **37** H1
Coppice Rd *KSCL* RG20 .... **9** H4
The Copse *TADY* RG26 .... **4** D3
Copse View Cl *CHIN* RG24 .... **20** B5
Cordale Rd *BSTK* RG21 .... **2** D7
Corinthian Cl *KEMP* RG22 .... **54** D3
Cornfields *AND* SP10 .... **56** C5
The Cornfields *KEMP* RG22 .... **54** D3
Cornish Cl *KEMP* RG22 .... **37** H4
Cornwallis Cl *ODIM* RG29 .... **43** H2
Coronation Rd *BSTK* RG21 .... **3** H1
Correlli Rd *KEMP* RG22 .... **55** G2
Corringway *FLET* GU13 .... **45** H1
Corunna Main *AND* SP10 .... **57** F3
Cotswold Cl *KEMP* RG22 .... **37** G3
Cottage Gn *HTWY* RG27 .... **22** B4
Cottington Cl *KSCL* RG20 .... **9** H4
Cottle Cl *BSTK* RG21 .... **38** D5
Council Rd *BSTK* RG21 .... **2** E6
Court Dro *OVTN* RG25 .... **49** H1
Courtmoor Av *FLET* GU13 .... **33** F5
Coventry Cl *KEMP* RG22 .... **54** C2
Cove Rd *FARN* GU14 .... **33** H1
Cowdray Pk *ALTN* GU34 .... **58** D5
Cowdrey Cl *BSTK* RG21 .... **27** F5
Cowdrey Hts *CHIN* RG24 .... **39** H1
Cowslip Bank *CHIN* RG24 .... **28** A5
Coxheath Rd *FLET* GU13 .... **45** E1
Crabs Hl *TADY* RG26 .... **10** C5
Crabtree Wy *CHIN* RG24 .... **40** C3
Cranbourne La *BSTK* RG21 .... **38** C5
Cranbrook Cl *FLET* GU13 .... **33** G1
Cranesfield *CHIN* RG24 .... **18** B5
Cranes Rd *CHIN* RG24 .... **18** B5
Cranford Av *FLET* GU13 .... **45** E2
Cranford Dr *ALTN* GU34 .... **59** G1
Crawts Rd *OVTN* RG25 .... **49** H3
The Crescent *AND* SP10 .... **56** A3
FLET GU13 .... **44** C1
Cress Gdns *AND* SP10 .... **56** D5
Crockford La *CHIN* RG24 .... **19** H5
Croft Av *AND* SP10 .... **57** E5
Crofters Meadow *CHIN* RG24 .... **28** A4
Croft Gdns *AND* SP10 .... **57** E5
Croft Rd *DEAN* RG23 .... **35** H5
The Crofts *KEMP* RG22 .... **54** D4
Cromwell Cl *BSTK* RG21 .... **40** C1
Cromwell Rd *BSTK* RG21 .... **2** D1
Crondall Rd *NFNM* GU10 .... **44** C5
Crookham Cl *TADY* RG26 .... **5** E5
Crookham Reach *FLET* GU13 .... **45** E2
Crookham Rd *FLET* GU13 .... **45** E1
Cropmark Wy *KEMP* RG22 .... **54** C3
Cross & Pillory La *ALTN* GU34 .... **58** D4
Crossborough Hl *BSTK* RG21 .... **3** H6
Cross La *AND* SP10 .... **56** D3
Cross St *BSTK* RG21 .... **2** E5
The Crossways *AND* SP10 .... **56** D3
Crowley Dr *ALTN* GU34 .... **59** E4
Crownfields *ODIM* RG29 .... **43** F3
Crown Gdns *FLET* GU13 .... **33** H4
Crown La *CHIN* RG24 .... **40** B1
Croye *AND* SP10 .... **56** D3
Cufaude La *TADY* RG26 .... **20** A3
Cuffelle Cl *CHIN* RG24 .... **28** B1
Culver Rd *BSTK* RG21 .... **38** D4
Cumberland Av *KEMP* RG22 .... **55** F1
Curlew Cl *KEMP* RG22 .... **54** B1
Curlews *ALTN* GU34 .... **58** D1
Curtis Rd *KEMP* RG22 .... **54** D4
Curzon Dr *FLET* GU13 .... **45** G2
Cusden Dr *AND* SP10 .... **57** E1
Cypress Gv *RAND* SP11 .... **56** A4
Cyprus Rd *KEMP* RG22 .... **54** D5

D

Daffodil Cl *KEMP* RG22 .... **54** B2
Dahlia Cl *KEMP* RG22 .... **54** B2
Dalewood *KEMP* RG22 .... **37** F5

Damsel Pth *BSTK* RG21 .... **3** K4
Dancers Meadow *CHIN* RG24 .... **26** C1
Dances Cl *AND* SP10 .... **57** F2
Dances La *WHCH* RG28 .... **47** F4
Danebury Rd *KEMP* RG22 .... **54** C4
Danehurst Pl *AND* SP10 .... **56** A3
Daneshill Dr *CHIN* RG24 .... **28** A4
Dankworth Rd *KEMP* RG22 .... **54** D2
Danvers Dr *FLET* GU13 .... **44** D3
Daphne Dr *FLET* GU13 .... **45** E4
Dark La *CHIN* RG24 .... **26** B1
Darset Av *FLET* GU13 .... **33** G2
Dart Ct *AND* SP10 .... **57** G1
Dashwood Cl *ALTN* GU34 .... **58** B5
Davy Cl *KEMP* RG22 .... **38** B2
Deane's Cl *BSTK* RG21 .... **3** C1
Deanswood Rd *TADY* RG26 .... **4** D3
Decouttere Cl *FLET* GU13 .... **45** E2
Deep La *BSTK* RG21 .... **2** A4
Delibes Rd *KEMP* RG22 .... **55** G2
Delius Cl *KEMP* RG22 .... **55** F1
Dellands *OVTN* RG25 .... **49** H3
Dellands La *OVTN* RG25 .... **49** G2
Dellfield *DEAN* RG23 .... **36** A4
Dell Rd *AND* SP10 .... **56** C2
The Dell *KSCL* RG20 .... **9** G4
Dene Ct *AND* SP10 .... **57** F4
Dene Rd *AND* SP10 .... **57** F4
Denham Dr *KEMP* RG22 .... **37** H5
Denmead Rd *TADY* RG26 .... **5** E3
Denning Cl *FLET* GU13 .... **33** E5
Deptford La *ODIM* RG29 .... **42** C2
Derby Flds *ODIM* RG29 .... **31** E4
Derwent Ct *AND* SP10 .... **57** G1
Derwent Rd *KEMP* RG22 .... **54** B1
Dever Wy *DEAN* RG23 .... **53** E1
Devonshire Pl *BSTK* RG21 .... **2** C6
Dewpond Wk *CHIN* RG24 .... **28** A4
Diana Cl *FLET* GU13 .... **38** B4
Dibley Cl *KEMP* RG22 .... **37** H4
Dickens La *CHIN* RG24 .... **40** B3
OVTN RG25 .... **40** A5
Dicker's La *ALTN* GU34 .... **59** E3
Dilly La *HTWY* RG27 .... **22** A5
Dinorben Av *FLET* GU13 .... **33** E5
Dinorben Beeches *FLET* GU13 .... **33** E5
Dinorben Cl *FLET* GU13 .... **33** F5
Divers Cl *ALTN* GU34 .... **58** D1
Dixon Rd *HTWY* RG27 .... **20** C1
Dominica Cl *CHIN* RG24 .... **27** F2
Dorchester Cl *DEAN* RG23 .... **37** G2
Dorchester Rd *HTWY* RG27 .... **30** C1
Dorchester Wy *ODIM* RG29 .... **42** B3
Dorrel Cl *KEMP* RG22 .... **54** C4
Doswell Wy *BSTK* RG21 .... **3** G1
Dove Cl *AND* SP10 .... **57** F1
KEMP RG22 .... **54** A1
Dover Cl *DEAN* RG23 .... **38** A1
Dowden Gv *ALTN* GU34 .... **58** D2
Down La *OVTN* RG25 .... **41** H5
Downsland Rd *BSTK* RG21 .... **2** B5
Downs Wy *ALTN* GU34 .... **58** B5
Dragonfly Dr *CHIN* RG24 .... **28** A4
Drayman's Wy *ALTN* GU34 .... **58** D4
Driftway Rd *HTWY* RG27 .... **31** E1
The Drive *BSTK* RG21 .... **53** E1
The Drove *AND* SP10 .... **56** B3
Droxford Crs *TADY* RG26 .... **4** D4
Dryden Cl *CHIN* RG24 .... **27** F4
Duchess Cl *ALTN* GU34 .... **58** C4
Duddon Wy *BSTK* RG21 .... **3** J4
Dudley Cl *DEAN* RG23 .... **37** G2
Dukes Cl *ALTN* GU34 .... **58** B5
Dukes Md *FLET* GU13 .... **32** D3
Dukes Ride *THLE* RG7 .... **6** C3
Du Maurier Cl *FLET* GU13 .... **45** E4
Dunley's Hl *ODIM* RG29 .... **43** E2
Dunmow Hl *FLET* GU13 .... **33** G2
Dunmow Rd *AND* SP10 .... **57** F5
Dunsford Crs *DEAN* RG23 .... **25** H5
Durham Wy *KEMP* RG22 .... **54** C2
Durley Cl *AND* SP10 .... **56** C4
Durnsford Av *FLET* GU13 .... **33** E5

E

Eagle Cl *ALTN* GU34 .... **58** D1
KEMP RG22 .... **54** A2
Eardley Av *AND* SP10 .... **56** B2
Earlsbourne *FLET* GU13 .... **45** H3
Eastbrooke Rd *ALTN* GU34 .... **59** E3
Eastern Av *AND* SP10 .... **57** F4
Eastfield Av *BSTK* RG21 .... **3** G4
Eastfield Cl *AND* SP10 .... **57** G3
Eastfield Rd *AND* SP10 .... **57** G3
Eastlyn Rd *TADY* RG26 .... **5** F1
East Portway *AND* SP10 .... **56** A3
Estrop La *BSTK* RG21 .... **3** G4
Eastrop Rbt *BSTK* RG21 .... **3** G3
Eastrop Wy *BSTK* RG21 .... **3** G3
East St *AND* SP10 .... **57** F4

Ecchinswell Rd *KSCL* RG20 ...... 9 E4
Edgehill Cl *KEMP* RG22 ...... 37 G4
Edney Cl *FLET* GU13 ...... 45 H1
Edward Rd *ALTN* GU34 ...... 59 E2
Eggars Cl *ALTN* GU34 ...... 59 F3
Eggleton Cl *FLET* GU13 ...... 45 E2 □
Elbow La *BSTK* RG21 ...... 2 E4
Elderberry Bank *CHIN* RG24 ...... 28 A4
Elgar Cl *KEMP* RG22 ...... 55 F2
Elizabeth Dr *FLET* GU13 ...... 45 G2
Elizabeth Rd *KEMP* RG22 ...... 38 B3
Ellen Gdns *TADY* RG26 ...... 15 H3
Ellington Dr *KEMP* RG22 ...... 54 D3
Elm Bank Rd *AND* SP10 ...... 57 E4
Elm Farm Gv *KSCL* RG20 ...... 9 G4 □
Elm Gv *KSCL* RG20 ...... 9 G4
Elmhurst *TADY* RG26 ...... 5 E4
Elm Rd *CHIN* RG24 ...... 26 A2
Elms Rd *HTWY* RG27 ...... 30 C1
The Elms *AND* SP10 ...... 56 D4
Elmwood Cl *ALTN* GU34 ...... 58 B5 □
Elmwood Wy *DEAN* RG23 ...... 25 H5
Elvetham Cl *FLET* GU13 ...... 33 F1
Elvetham La *HTWY* RG27 ...... 22 D1
Elvetham Pl *HTWY* RG27 ...... 33 E1
Elvetham Rd *FLET* GU13 ...... 32 D2
Ennerdale Cl *KEMP* RG22 ...... 37 G5
Enterprise Ct *CHIN* RG24 ...... 27 G5
Epsom Down *ALTN* GU34 ...... 58 D5
Erskine Cl *TADY* RG26 ...... 5 E2
Esher Cl *KEMP* RG22 ...... 55 E1
Essex Rd *BSTK* RG21 ...... 2 D4
Eton Cl *KEMP* RG22 ...... 54 B4
Euskirchen Wy *KEMP* RG22 ...... 37 H2
Eversfield Cl *AND* SP10 ...... 56 D3
Evingar Gdns *WHCH* RG28 ...... 47 F4
Evingar Rd *WHCH* RG28 ...... 47 F4
Ewhurst Rd *TADY* RG26 ...... 16 B2
Ewshot La *FLET* GU13 ...... 45 F1
Exbury Wy *AND* SP10 ...... 56 C4
Exeter Cl *KEMP* RG22 ...... 54 C3
Exmoor Cl *KEMP* RG22 ...... 37 G4

F

Fairfield *WHCH* RG28 ...... 47 F4
Fairfields Rd *BSTK* RG21 ...... 2 E7
Fairland Cl *FLET* GU13 ...... 33 H4
Fairlawn Rd *TADY* RG26 ...... 5 G4
Fairmile *FLET* GU13 ...... 45 G1
Fairoak Wy *TADY* RG26 ...... 4 A2
Fairthorne Ri *CHIN* RG24 ...... 40 D2 □
Fairview Meadow *DEAN* RG23 ...... 53 F2
Falcon Cl *KEMP* RG22 ...... 54 A1
Falcon Flds *TADY* RG26 ...... 5 E1
Falkland Rd *CHIN* RG24 ...... 27 F2
Fantails *ALTN* GU34 ...... 58 D1
Faraday Rd *CHIN* RG24 ...... 27 G4
Farleigh Ri *BSTK* RG21 ...... 39 F5
Farm Ground Cl *HTWY* RG27 ...... 31 E1 □
Farmhouse Wy *FLET* GU13 ...... 45 E3
Farm View Dr *CHIN* RG24 ...... 28 B1
Farnham Rd *ODIM* RG29 ...... 43 H2
Faroe Cl *CHIN* RG24 ...... 27 G3
Farringdon Wy *TADY* RG26 ...... 5 E4
Farrs Av *AND* SP10 ...... 57 F5
Fawconer Rd *KSCL* RG20 ...... 9 G4
Fayrewood Cha *KEMP* RG22 ...... 54 C3 □
Feathers La *BSTK* RG21 ...... 3 F5
Feld Wy *CHIN* RG24 ...... 28 B5
Fennel Cl *CHIN* RG24 ...... 20 B4
Ferbies *FLET* GU13 ...... 45 G1
Ferguson Cl *BSTK* RG21 ...... 38 D5
Ferndale Rd *AND* SP10 ...... 56 C2
  FLET GU13 ...... 45 E2
Fern Dr *FLET* GU13 ...... 45 E1
Ferrell Fld *HTWY* RG27 ...... 30 B1
Fielders Cl *ALTN* GU34 ...... 58 D4
Field Gate Dr *KSCL* RG20 ...... 9 F4
Fieldway *FLET* GU13 ...... 32 D4 □
Finch Cl *TADY* RG26 ...... 5 F4 □
Finches Gn *ALTN* GU34 ...... 58 D1
Fingle Dr *AND* SP10 ...... 56 C3
Fir Cl *FLET* GU13 ...... 33 F4
Firecrest Rd *KEMP* RG22 ...... 54 A4
Fire Thorn Cl *FLET* GU13 ...... 45 F1
Firs La *ODIM* RG29 ...... 43 E3
First Av *THLE* RG7 ...... 5 F1
Firs Wy *DEAN* RG23 ...... 25 G5
  WHCH RG28 ...... 47 F5
Firth Cl *THLE* RG7 ...... 6 C5
Firtree Wy *FLET* GU13 ...... 33 H4
Fiske Cl *KEMP* RG22 ...... 37 H5
Fitzroy Rd *FLET* GU13 ...... 32 D3
Flaxfield Ct *BSTK* RG21 ...... 2 D4
Flaxfield Rd *BSTK* RG21 ...... 2 D4
Fleet Rd *FLET* GU13 ...... 33 F3
  HTWY RG27 ...... 23 E4
Fletcher Cl *BSTK* RG21 ...... 2 D6
Flint Cl *AND* SP10 ...... 56 B5
Floral Wy *AND* SP10 ...... 56 B5

Florence Portal Cl *WHCH* RG28 ...... 48 C5
Florence Rd *FLET* GU13 ...... 45 H1
Florence Wy *CHIN* RG24 ...... 25 H4
Focus Wy *AND* SP10 ...... 57 H2
Folly Cl *FLET* GU13 ...... 33 G5
Fontwell Dr *ALTN* GU34 ...... 58 D5
Ford La *ODIM* RG29 ...... 42 B5
Forest Cl *TADY* RG26 ...... 4 B2
Forest Dr *CHIN* RG24 ...... 20 A5
Forest End *FLET* GU13 ...... 45 F1
Forest La *TADY* RG26 ...... 5 F1
Forth Ct *AND* SP10 ...... 57 G1 □
Fountains Cl *KEMP* RG22 ...... 54 A3
Four Acre Coppice
  HTWY RG27 ...... 31 E1 □
Four Lanes Cl *CHIN* RG24 ...... 28 B1
Foxcotte Cl *AND* SP10 ...... 56 B1
Fox Cft *FLET* GU13 ...... 45 G2
Foxglove Cl *KEMP* RG22 ...... 54 B3
Fox La *DEAN* RG23 ...... 36 B4
Foxmoor Cl *DEAN* RG23 ...... 36 A4
Foxs Furlong *CHIN* RG24 ...... 20 C5
Fox's La *KSCL* RG20 ...... 9 F5
Foye La *FLET* GU13 ...... 45 H2
Foyle Pk *BSTK* RG21 ...... 39 E5
Frances Rd *BSTK* RG21 ...... 2 D6
Franklin Av *HTWY* RG27 ...... 22 A2
  TADY RG26 ...... 4 D2
Fraser Cl *CHIN* RG24 ...... 40 D1
Freelands Dr *FLET* GU13 ...... 45 E2
Freemantle Cl *BSTK* RG21 ...... 27 C5
Frere Av *FLET* GU13 ...... 33 E5
Frescade Crs *BSTK* RG21 ...... 2 C7
Frithmead Cl *BSTK* RG21 ...... 38 D5
Frog La *OVTN* RG25 ...... 41 G2
  TADY RG26 ...... 5 F5
Frogs Hole *KSCL* RG20 ...... 9 F5
Frome Cl *BSTK* RG21 ...... 3 J3
  DEAN RG23 ...... 53 F1
Froud Cl *HTWY* RG27 ...... 30 B2 □
Fulbrook Wy *ODIM* RG29 ...... 43 F5
Fullerton Wy *TADY* RG26 ...... 5 F4
Fulmar Cl *KEMP* RG22 ...... 54 A3
Further Vell-Mead *FLET* GU13 ...... 45 E3
Furze Rd *TADY* RG26 ...... 4 C1
Fuzzy Dro *KEMP* RG22 ...... 54 A2
Fylingdales Cl *KEMP* RG22 ...... 37 F5

G

Gables Rd *FLET* GU13 ...... 45 F3
Gage Cl *CHIN* RG24 ...... 28 A5
Gainsborough Rd *BSTK* RG21 ...... 39 F5
Galahad Cl *AND* SP10 ...... 57 E1
Galloway Cl *KEMP* RG22 ...... 37 G4
Gally Hill Rd *FLET* GU13 ...... 45 F3
Gander Dr *CHIN* RG24 ...... 25 H4
Gannet Cl *KEMP* RG22 ...... 54 A3
Garden Cl *HTWY* RG27 ...... 30 B1 □
  KSCL RG20 ...... 9 G4 □
Garrett Cl *KSCL* RG20 ...... 9 F3
Gaskell Cl *ALTN* GU34 ...... 59 C1
Gauvain Cl *ALTN* GU34 ...... 59 E5
Geale's Crs *ALTN* GU34 ...... 59 E2
George Rd *FLET* GU13 ...... 33 H3
George St *BSTK* RG21 ...... 2 B4
  KSCL RG20 ...... 9 F4
George Yd *AND* SP10 ...... 57 F3
Georgia Cl *AND* SP10 ...... 56 B5
Georgia Gdns *TADY* RG26 ...... 5 H3
Gerald Sq *ALTN* GU34 ...... 59 E1
Gershwin Rd *KEMP* RG22 ...... 54 F2
Gilbard Ct *CHIN* RG24 ...... 28 B1 □
Gilbert White Wy *ALTN* GU34 ...... 58 D2
Giles Rd *TADY* RG26 ...... 5 F3
Gillies Dr *CHIN* RG24 ...... 25 H4
Glade Cl *CHIN* RG24 ...... 28 A2
Glamis Cl *DEAN* RG23 ...... 35 H5
Glastonbury Cl *CHIN* RG24 ...... 26 D4
Glebe Cl *TADY* RG26 ...... 5 F4
Glebe Ct *FLET* GU13 ...... 33 F3
Glebe La *DEAN* RG23 ...... 37 F3
  HTWY RG27 ...... 22 B4
Glebe Meadow *OVTN* RG25 ...... 49 H2
Glen Cl *AND* SP10 ...... 56 C3
Glendale Pk *FLET* GU13 ...... 32 C2
Glendale Rd *TADY* RG26 ...... 4 D2
Glen Rd *FLET* GU13 ...... 33 H4
The Glen *TADY* RG26 ...... 5 H2
Gloucester Dr *KEMP* RG22 ...... 54 B5
Goat La *BSTK* RG21 ...... 3 G4
Goch Wy *AND* SP10 ...... 56 C1
Goddards Cl *HTWY* RG27 ...... 21 E1 □
Goddards Firs *DEAN* RG23 ...... 53 F2
Goddards Md *AND* SP10 ...... 56 C4 □
Goddard Sq *AND* SP10 ...... 57 F1
Gondreville Gdns *FLET* GU13 ...... 45 E3
Goodman Cl *BSTK* RG21 ...... 2 A6
Goodwood Cl *ALTN* GU34 ...... 58 D5
Goodyers *ALTN* GU34 ...... 59 E4
Gordon Av *FLET* GU13 ...... 45 H1

Gordon Cl *BSTK* RG21 ...... 3 H1
Gorselands *TADY* RG26 ...... 5 F3
Gorseway *FLET* GU13 ...... 33 G5
Gough Rd *FLET* GU13 ...... 33 E2
Gower Cl *BSTK* RG21 ...... 3 K1
Gower Crs *HTWY* RG27 ...... 30 D1 □
Gracemere Crs *KEMP* RG22 ...... 54 A3
Grace Sq *AND* SP10 ...... 57 G1
Grafton Wy *KEMP* RG22 ...... 38 A3
Grainger Cl *KEMP* RG22 ...... 55 F1
Grampian Wy *KEMP* RG22 ...... 37 G4
Granada Pl *AND* SP10 ...... 57 G2
Grange Rd *FLET* GU13 ...... 45 F2
Grantley Dr *FLET* GU13 ...... 33 F5
Gravelly Cl *TADY* RG26 ...... 5 F5
Gravel Rd *FLET* GU13 ...... 45 H1
Great Binfields Crs *CHIN* RG24 ...... 28 A4
Great Binfields Rd *CHIN* RG24 ...... 28 A5
Great La *WHCH* RG28 ...... 47 F5
Great Oaks Cha *CHIN* RG24 ...... 27 H2 □
Great Sheldons Coppice
  HTWY RG27 ...... 30 B1
Grebe Cl *ALTN* GU34 ...... 58 C1
  KEMP RG22 ...... 54 A3
Greenacre *KSCL* RG20 ...... 9 G4 □
Greenbirch Cl *KEMP* RG22 ...... 54 A3
Greenbury Cl *DEAN* RG23 ...... 37 H2
Greenfields Av *ALTN* GU34 ...... 58 C3
Green Glades *FLET* GU13 ...... 45 F2
Greenhaven Cl *AND* SP10 ...... 57 G4 □
Greenlands Rd *KSCL* RG20 ...... 9 G4
Green La *HTWY* RG27 ...... 22 A4
  TADY RG26 ...... 5 F5
Green Leys *FLET* GU13 ...... 45 F3
The Green *AND* SP10 ...... 56 C1 □
  OVTN RG25 ...... 50 A2
  TADY RG26 ...... 5 F5
  WHCH RG28 ...... 47 G5
Greenway *HTWY* RG27 ...... 21 E1
Greenways *FLET* GU13 ...... 45 F1
Greenwich Wy *AND* SP10 ...... 57 G1
Greenwood Dr *CHIN* RG24 ...... 20 A5 □
Greenwoods *WHCH* RG28 ...... 47 F4
Gregory Cl *BSTK* RG21 ...... 27 F5
Greig Rd *KEMP* RG22 ...... 55 F1
Grenville Dr *FLET* GU13 ...... 33 E5
Gresley Rd *BSTK* RG21 ...... 3 K1
  CHIN RG24 ...... 27 G5
Greyhound La *OVTN* RG25 ...... 49 H3
Greywell Cl *TADY* RG26 ...... 4 D3 □
Greywell Rd *CHIN* RG24 ...... 41 E2
Griffin Wy South *HTWY* RG27 ...... 31 E1
Grosvenor Cl *KEMP* RG22 ...... 54 C5 □
Grove Cl *BSTK* RG21 ...... 39 F4
Grove Rd *ALTN* GU34 ...... 58 D5
  BSTK RG21 ...... 39 F5
  FLET GU13 ...... 45 H2
Guernsey Cl *CHIN* RG24 ...... 27 F2
Guinea Ct *CHIN* RG24 ...... 28 B1 □
Guttridge La *TADY* RG26 ...... 4 D3

H

Hackwood Cl *AND* SP10 ...... 56 B4 □
Hackwood Rd *BSTK* RG21 ...... 3 F6
Hackwood Road Rbt *BSTK* RG21 ...... 3 G7
Hadleigh Pl *BSTK* RG21 ...... 2 D4
Hadrians Wy *DEAN* RG23 ...... 25 H5 □
Hagley Rd *FLET* GU13 ...... 33 E2
Haig La *FLET* GU13 ...... 45 H2
Haig Rd *AND* SP10 ...... 56 D4
Hailstone Rd *BSTK* RG21 ...... 27 E4
Halifax Cl *AND* SP10 ...... 56 D2
Halliday Cl *BSTK* RG21 ...... 38 D5
Hall Rd *ALTN* GU34 ...... 59 E1
Hamble Cl *DEAN* RG23 ...... 53 E1 □
Hamble Ct *BSTK* RG21 ...... 3 K4
Hamble Dr *TADY* RG26 ...... 5 G3
Hamelyn Rd *BSTK* RG21 ...... 2 C6
Hamilton Rd *FLET* GU13 ...... 45 H1 □
Ham La *TADY* RG26 ...... 11 G2
Hammond Rd *BSTK* RG21 ...... 2 D7
Hampshire Cl *KEMP* RG22 ...... 37 F4
Hampton Cl *FLET* GU13 ...... 45 G3
Handel Cl *KEMP* RG22 ...... 55 F1
Hanger Rd *TADY* RG26 ...... 4 C2
Hangers Wy *ALTN* GU34 ...... 59 E3
Hanmore Rd *CHIN* RG24 ...... 27 H2
Hanover Cl *AND* SP10 ...... 56 B5 □
Hanover Gdns *BSTK* RG21 ...... 38 B5
Hanson Rd *ALTN* GU34 ...... 56 C2
Hardings La *HTWY* RG27 ...... 22 B3 □
Hardy La *BSTK* RG21 ...... 2 A7
Hardys Fld *KSCL* RG20 ...... 9 F3
Harebell Cl *HTWY* RG27 ...... 22 B2 □
Harebell Gdns *HTWY* RG27 ...... 22 B2
Hare's La *HTWY* RG27 ...... 22 B2
Harfield Cl *HTWY* RG27 ...... 30 C1 □
Harlech Cl *DEAN* RG23 ...... 37 H2
Harlington Wy *FLET* GU13 ...... 33 E4
Harmsworth Rd *TADY* RG26 ...... 5 E3 □

Harold Gdns *ALTN* GU34 ...... 59 E2
Harris Hl *KEMP* RG22 ...... 54 C3
Harroway *WHCH* RG28 ...... 47 E1
Harrow Wy *AND* SP10 ...... 56 B2
  OVTN RG25 ...... 34 C4
The Harrow Wy *KEMP* RG22 ...... 55 F1
Hartford Ct *HTWY* RG27 ...... 22 A3 □
Hartford Rd *HTWY* RG27 ...... 22 A3
Hartley Gdns *TADY* RG26 ...... 5 E4
Hartley Meadow *WHCH* RG28 ...... 47 E5 □
Hartleys *THLE* RG7 ...... 6 B3
Hartshill Rd *TADY* RG26 ...... 4 C3
Hartsleaf Cl *FLET* GU13 ...... 33 F4 □
Hartswood *CHIN* RG24 ...... 27 H2
Harvest Wy *CHIN* RG24 ...... 28 A4
Harveys Fld *OVTN* RG25 ...... 49 H2
Hastings Cl *DEAN* RG23 ...... 37 G2
Hatch La *CHIN* RG24 ...... 40 C2
Hatchwarren Gdns
  KEMP RG22 ...... 55 F3 □
Hatchwarren La *KEMP* RG22 ...... 54 D3
Hatch Warren La *KEMP* RG22 ...... 55 G1
Hathaway Gdns *CHIN* RG24 ...... 27 F4
Hattem Pl *AND* SP10 ...... 56 D1 □
Hawk Cl *KEMP* RG22 ...... 54 A2 □
Hawkes Cl *HTWY* RG27 ...... 22 A2
Hawkfield La *BSTK* RG21 ...... 2 D6
Hawkins Gv *FLET* GU13 ...... 44 D1
Hawkley Dr *TADY* RG26 ...... 5 F4
Hawkwell *FLET* GU13 ...... 45 H3
Hawthorns *ALTN* GU34 ...... 58 C2
The Hawthorns *TADY* RG26 ...... 4 B5 □
Hawthorn Wy *DEAN* RG23 ...... 37 H1
Haydn Rd *KEMP* RG22 ...... 55 E2
Haydock Cl *ALTN* GU34 ...... 58 D5
Haywarden Pl *HTWY* RG27 ...... 22 B2
Haywood Dr *FLET* GU13 ...... 33 G5
Hazel Cl *AND* SP10 ...... 56 B5
  DEAN RG23 ...... 53 E1
Hazeldene *CHIN* RG24 ...... 28 A2 □
Hazeley Cl *HTWY* RG27 ...... 22 A2
Hazel Gn *TADY* RG26 ...... 4 A2 □
Hazelwood Cl *DEAN* RG23 ...... 26 A5
Hazelwood Dr *DEAN* RG23 ...... 26 A5
Hazely Cl *HTWY* RG27 ...... 22 A2
Headington Cl *KEMP* RG22 ...... 55 E2 □
Heath End Rd *TADY* RG26 ...... 4 B2
Heather Dr *AND* SP10 ...... 56 D2
  FLET GU13 ...... 45 E2
  TADY RG26 ...... 4 C1
Heather Gv *HTWY* RG27 ...... 22 A2
Heather Wy *KEMP* RG22 ...... 54 B3
Heathfield Ct *FLET* GU13 ...... 45 E1
Heathfield Rd *KEMP* RG22 ...... 54 B3
Heathlands *TADY* RG26 ...... 4 B2 □
Heath Rd *TADY* RG26 ...... 5 H2
Heathrow Copse *TADY* RG26 ...... 4 A3
Heath V *AND* SP10 ...... 57 F4
Hedge End Rd *AND* SP10 ...... 57 F5
The Hedgerows *CHIN* RG24 ...... 28 B4
Hedges Md *AND* SP10 ...... 56 D5
Hele Cl *BSTK* RG21 ...... 38 D5
Helford Ct *AND* SP10 ...... 57 G1 □
Hendren Sq *AND* SP10 ...... 57 G1 🔟
Hepplewhite Cl *TADY* RG26 ...... 4 B3
Hepplewhite Dr *KEMP* RG22 ...... 54 B3
Hepworth Cl *AND* SP10 ...... 57 E2
Herbert Rd *FLET* GU13 ...... 33 E3
Hereford Cl *ODIM* RG29 ...... 43 E3 □
Hereford Rd *DEAN* RG23 ...... 37 H2
Heritage Pk *DEAN* RG23 ...... 37 G2
Heron La *FLET* GU13 ...... 58 D1
Heron Pk *CHIN* RG24 ...... 28 C3
Herons Ri *ALTN* GU34 ...... 57 F5
Heron Wy *KEMP* RG22 ...... 54 A2
Herriard Wy *TADY* RG26 ...... 5 E4 □
Highams Cl *KSCL* RG20 ...... 9 G4
Highdown *FLET* GU13 ...... 33 G2
Highdowns *KEMP* RG22 ...... 54 D4
High Dr *KEMP* RG22 ...... 37 H5
Higher Md *CHIN* RG24 ...... 28 A4
Highfield Cha *BSTK* RG21 ...... 2 B4
Highland Dr *DEAN* RG23 ...... 35 H5
  FARN GU14 ...... 33 H1
Highlands Rd *AND* SP10 ...... 57 G4
  KEMP RG22 ...... 54 C4
Highmoors *CHIN* RG24 ...... 27 H1
Highridge *ALTN* GU34 ...... 58 D4
High St *ALTN* GU34 ...... 58 D4
  AND SP10 ...... 57 F3
  HTWY RG27 ...... 22 B3
  ODIM RG29 ...... 43 F3
  OVTN RG25 ...... 49 H2
Highwood Rdg *KEMP* RG22 ...... 54 C4
Hillary Rd *BSTK* RG21 ...... 26 C5
Hillbury Av *AND* SP10 ...... 56 C5
Hillcrest *FLET* GU13 ...... 33 G1 □
Hillcrest Ct *DEAN* RG23 ...... 37 G1 □
Hill Rd *DEAN* RG23 ...... 52 D1
Hillside *TADY* RG26 ...... 12 A2
Hillside Cl *ALTN* GU34 ...... 58 D2 □
  FLET GU13 ...... 44 C1
Hillside Rd *ODIM* RG29 ...... 43 H4
Hill View Rd *KEMP* RG22 ...... 38 B4

Hinton Cl TADY RG26 5 E4
Hitches La FLET GU13 32 C5
Hobbs Sq AND SP10 57 G1
Hogarth Cl BSTK RG21 39 H3
Hogarth Ct AND SP10 56 D2
Holbein Cl BSTK RG21 39 G4
Holland Gdns FLET GU13 33 G4
Hollowshot La KSCL RG20 9 F5
Hollybush La TADY RG26 12 C4
Holly Dr CHIN RG24 40 D1
Hollyhock Cl KEMP RG22 54 B2
Holly La THLE RG7 6 C3
Hollytrees FLET GU13 45 E1
Holmes Cl KEMP RG22 54 D4 2
Holmes Ct AND SP10 56 C4 4
Holst Cl KEMP RG22 55 F3
Holt La HTWY RG27 31 E3
TADY RG26 11 E2
Holy Barn Cl KEMP RG22 54 B1
Home Farm Rd HTWY RG27 23 F2
Homesteads Rd KEMP RG22 54 B1
Honeybottom Rd TADY RG26 5 E2
Honeysuckle Cl KEMP RG22 54 B2 2
Hook Common HTWY RG27 30 B3
Hook Rd HTWY RG27 30 C3
KSCL RG20 9 H4
ODIM RG29 31 E5
ODIM RG29 42 B1
Hoopersmead OVTN RG25 55 H3
Hoopers Wy DEAN RG23 53 E1
Hopfield Rd HTWY RG27 22 A4
Hop Gdn FLET GU13 45 E3
Hop Garden Rd HTWY RG27 30 B1
Hopton Garth CHIN RG24 28 B3
Horwood Gdns BSTK RG21 38 C5
Houndmills Rd BSTK RG21 38 B1
Howard Rd BSTK RG21 39 F4 3
Howes Gdns FLET GU13 45 E1
Hubbard Rd BSTK RG21 26 C5
Huish La OVTN RG25 40 C5
Hulbert Wy KEMP RG22 37 H5
Humber Ct AND SP10 57 G1 11
Humberstone Rd AND SP10 57 E5
Hunnels Cl FLET GU13 45 E4
Hunters Cl DEAN RG23 36 A4
Hunts Cl HTWY RG27 31 E1 3
Huntsmead ALTN GU34 59 E4
Huntsmoor Rd TADY RG26 4 C3
Hutton Sq AND SP10 57 G1
Hyacinth Cl KEMP RG22 54 B2 3
Hydes Platt THLE RG7 6 C3

I

Ilex Cl TADY RG26 5 H2
Impstone Rd TADY RG26 6 A2
Inglewood Dr KEMP RG22 54 C4
Inhams Rd ALTN GU34 59 H1
Inhams Wy THLE RG7 6 B3
Inhurst Wy TADY RG26 4 C2
Inkpen Gdns CHIN RG24 28 B4
Iris Cl KEMP RG22 54 B3
Irwell Cl BSTK RG21 3 J4
Itchen Cl DEAN RG23 53 E1
Itchen Ct AND SP10 57 G1
Ivar Gdns CHIN RG24 28 B4
Ivy Down La DEAN RG23 35 F4
Ivyhole Hl HTWY RG27 23 F1

J

Jackdaw Cl KEMP RG22 54 A2
James Cl BSTK RG21 27 F5
Jardine Sq AND SP10 57 G1 12
Jasmine Rd KEMP RG22 54 C2
Jays Cl KEMP RG22 55 H1
Jefferson Rd BSTK RG21 27 E5
Jenner Wy ALTN GU34 59 E1
Jenson Gdns AND SP10 56 C4
Jersey Cl CHIN RG24 27 F2
Jessett Dr FLET GU13 45 E3
Jobson Cl WHCH RG28 47 F5 2
Johnson Wy FLET GU13 45 F1
Joule Rd BSTK RG21 26 C5
Jubilee Cl TADY RG26 5 H2
Jubilee Rd BSTK RG21 2 E6
Julius Cl CHIN RG24 25 H4
Junction Rd AND SP10 56 D3
June Dr DEAN RG23 37 G2
Juniper Cl CHIN RG24 20 B5

K

Kathleen Cl BSTK RG21 38 D5 2
Keats Cl CHIN RG24 27 F3
Keeps Md KSCL RG20 9 F3
Kellynch Cl ALTN GU34 58 C3
Kellys Wk AND SP10 56 C4
Kelvin Hl KEMP RG22 38 B5
Kemmitt Wy AND SP10 56 C5 1
Kempshott Gdns KEMP RG22 54 B2 4
Kempshott Gv KEMP RG22 37 F3 1
Kempshott La KEMP RG22 54 B1
Kempton Cl ALTN GU34 58 D5
Kendal Gdns KEMP RG22 54 C1
Kenilworth Rd DEAN RG23 37 G1 2
FLET GU13 33 H3
Kenmore Cl FLET GU13 45 H2
Kennet Cl BSTK RG21 3 J4
Kennet Ct AND SP10 57 G1
Kennet Wy DEAN RG23 53 E1
Kent Rd FLET GU13 33 H3
Kenyons Yd AND SP10 56 C3
Kerchers Fld OVTN RG25 49 H3
Kerfield Wy HTWY RG27 30 D1 3
Kersley Crs ODIM RG29 43 E5
Kestrel Rd KEMP RG22 54 A1
Ketelbey Ri KEMP RG22 55 G3
Kevin Cl KSCL RG20 10 A4
Kevins Gv FLET GU13 33 H3
Kew Wk AND SP10 56 C4
Keynes Cl FLET GU13 45 H3
Kiln Gdns HTWY RG27 22 A3
Kiln La TADY RG26 17 F4
Kiln Rd CHIN RG24 26 B1
Kimbell Rd KEMP RG22 38 C5
Kimber Cl CHIN RG24 28 A2
Kimberley FLET GU13 45 H3
Kimberley Cl AND SP10 56 B1 1
Kimberley Rd KEMP RG22 38 B4
Kimbers La TADY RG26 13 G1
Kingfisher Cl FLET GU13 45 G2
KEMP RG22 54 A1
King George Rd AND SP10 56 B3
King John Rd KSCL RG20 9 G4
King Johns Rd ODIM RG29 43 E1
Kingsclere Rd BSTK RG21 2 B1
DEAN RG23 24 D2
OVTN RG25 49 H2
Kingscroft FLET GU13 33 G4
Kings Furlong Dr BSTK RG21 2 B7
Kings Keep FLET GU13 45 G1
Kingsland Rd ALTN GU34 58 C4
Kingsley Pk WHCH RG28 47 F4
Kingsmead ALTN GU34 58 D4
Kings Meadow AND SP10 57 F4 1
OVTN RG25 49 H2
Kingsmill Rd BSTK RG21 38 D5
Kings Orch DEAN RG23 53 E2
Kings Pightle CHIN RG24 28 A1
Kings Rd ALTN GU34 58 B5
FLET GU13 33 H3
KEMP RG22 38 B4
THLE RG7 6 B2
Kingston Cl AND SP10 56 C5
King St ODIM RG29 43 G2
Kings Wk WHCH RG28 47 F5
King's Yd AND SP10 57 F3
Kintyre Cl DEAN RG23 35 H5
Kipling Wk KEMP RG22 38 B4
Knapp La TADY RG26 5 G5
Knight Cl FLET GU13 44 C1
Knight St BSTK RG21 2 A6
Knights Wy ALTN GU34 58 B4
Knoll Cl FLET GU13 33 G2
Knoll Rd FLET GU13 33 G2
Knollys Rd THLE RG7 6 A2
Knowle Crs KSCL RG20 9 G4
Knox Cl FLET GU13 44 D2

L

Laburnum Wy DEAN RG23 38 A1
Laffans Rd ODIM RG29 43 F5
Lakelands TADY RG26 4 A2 2
Laker Sq AND SP10 57 G1
Lakeside Cl AND SP10 56 B1
Lakeside Ct FARN GU14 33 H1
Lamb Cl AND SP10 57 G4
Lambdens Wk TADY RG26 5 E3 2
Lambs Rw CHIN RG24 28 A5
Lancaster Cl AND SP10 56 D2 1
Lancaster Rd BSTK RG21 2 C1
Landseer Cl BSTK RG21 39 G4
Landseer Ct AND SP10 57 E2 1
The Lane TADY RG26 5 E3
Langham Rd ALTN GU34 58 C4
Langley Cl FLET GU13 45 F3
Lansdowne Av AND SP10 56 C5
Lansdowne Rd ALTN GU34 59 E2
Lansley Rd BSTK RG21 27 E4 1
Lapin La KEMP RG22 54 C5
Lapwing Ri WHCH RG28 47 E4
Larch Dr AND SP10 56 A4
KSCL RG20 9 G4
Larchfield Rd FLET GU13 33 G5
Larchwood CHIN RG24 28 A1 2
Lark Cl AND SP10 57 F1
KEMP RG22 54 A2
Larkfield CHIN RG24 28 A1
Larmer Cl FLET GU13 32 D5
Larwood Sq AND SP10 57 G1 13
Laurel Cl ODIM RG29 43 E2
The Laurels AND SP10 56 C2
BSTK RG21 3 H1
FLET GU13 33 G3
Lavender Rd KEMP RG22 54 B3
Laverstoke La WHCH RG28 48 D5
Lawrence Cl AND SP10 56 D1
CHIN RG24 27 F3
Lawrencedale Ct BSTK RG21 2 B5
Lawrence Rd FLET GU13 33 F4
Lay Fld HTWY RG27 30 B1
Lea Cl BSTK RG21 3 K3
Lea Springs FLET GU13 32 D5
The Lea FLET GU13 32 D5
Leawood Rd FLET GU13 32 D5 1
Le Borowe FLET GU13 45 E3
Lefroy Av BSTK RG21 27 F5
Leger Cl FLET GU13 45 E2
Lehar Cl KEMP RG22 55 E2
Leicester Pl AND SP10 57 E4 2
Leigh Cl AND SP10 57 G4
Leigh Gdns AND SP10 57 G4
Leigh Rd AND SP10 57 G4
Leipzig Barracks FLET GU13 45 H5
Leipzig Rd FLET GU13 45 H4
Lennon Wy KEMP RG22 54 D3
Lenten St ALTN GU34 58 C4
Levignen Cl FLET GU13 44 D2
Lewis Cl BSTK RG21 27 F5
Leyton Wy RAND SP11 56 C5
Lightfoot Gv BSTK RG21 39 E5
Lightsfield DEAN RG23 36 A5
Lilac Wy DEAN RG23 38 A1
Lily Cl KEMP RG22 54 B3
Lime Av ALTN GU34 58 C2
Lime Gv ALTN GU34 58 C2
Lime Tree Wy CHIN RG24 27 H1
Lincoln Cl KEMP RG22 54 C3
Lincoln Gn ALTN GU34 58 C5
Linden Av CHIN RG24 40 C2
ODIM RG29 43 H1
The Lines KSCL RG20 9 G3
Lingfield Cl CHIN RG24 40 D2
Lingmala Gv FLET GU13 45 H2 2
Link Rd ALTN GU34 59 E1
KSCL RG20 9 H4
The Link AND SP10 56 A3
Link Wy DEAN RG23 53 E1
Linkway FLET GU13 45 F1
Linnet Cl KEMP RG22 37 F5
Linnets Wy ALTN GU34 58 D2
Linton Cl TADY RG26 5 F4
Linton Dr AND SP10 56 D2
Lion Cl OVTN RG25 49 H3
Lion Wy FLET GU13 45 H2
Lipscombe Ri ALTN GU34 58 D2
Lismoyne Cl FLET GU13 33 F2 1
Lister Rd KEMP RG22 38 B5
Little Basing CHIN RG24 28 A5
Little Copse AND SP10 56 C5 2
FLET GU13 33 F5
Little Copse Cha CHIN RG24 27 H2
Little Fallow CHIN RG24 28 A4
Littlefield Rd ALTN GU34 59 E3
Little Knowle Hl KSCL RG20 10 A2
Little London Rd THLE RG7 6 B5
Litton Gdns DEAN RG23 53 E1
Locksbridge La TADY RG26 15 G4
Lock Sq AND SP10 57 G1
Loddon Dr BSTK RG21 3 J4
Lodge Cl AND SP10 56 C3 1
Loggon Rd BSTK RG21 55 H1
Lomond Cl DEAN RG23 52 D1
Londlandes FLET GU13 45 E3
London Rd ALTN GU34 59 F2
AND SP10 57 H3
BSTK RG21 3 F5
CHIN RG24 40 C3
HTWY RG27 22 A4 2
HTWY RG27 29 H5
ODIM RG29 43 G2
OVTN RG25 49 G3
WHCH RG28 47 H5
London St WHCH RG28 47 F5
Longacre Ri CHIN RG24 27 H2 2
Long Copse Cha CHIN RG24 27 H2
Longcroft Rd KSCL RG20 9 F3
Long Cross La KEMP RG22 54 B4
Longdown FLET GU13 45 F1
Long Gv TADY RG26 4 A1
Long La CHIN RG24 28 B2
ODIM RG29 43 H5
Longmead FLET GU13 45 G1
Longmoor Rd BSTK RG21 2 C6
Longs Ct WHCH RG28 47 F5 3
Longstock Cl AND SP10 56 C4 5
CHIN RG24 20 C5
Lordsfield Gdns OVTN RG25 49 G2
Lordswood THLE RG7 6 B3
Lovegroves CHIN RG24 28 B1
Love La AND SP10 57 F4
KSCL RG20 9 G4
ODIM RG29 43 F4
Loveridge Cl BSTK RG21 38 D5
Lower Brook St BSTK RG21 2 A4
Lower Evingar Rd WHCH RG28 47 F5
Lower Turk St ALTN GU34 58 D4
Lower Wote St BSTK RG21 3 F3
Lowlands Rd KEMP RG22 37 F4
Lowry Ct AND SP10 56 D2 2
Loxwood Av FLET GU13 33 E5
Loyalty La CHIN RG24 40 C1
Ludlow Cl DEAN RG23 37 H2
Ludlow Gdns DEAN RG23 38 A2
Lundy Cl CHIN RG24 27 G3
Lune Cl BSTK RG21 3 J4
Lune Ct AND SP10 57 G1
Lupin Cl KEMP RG22 54 B2
Lutyens Cl CHIN RG24 28 A4
Lyde Cl DEAN RG23 53 E1
Lyford Rd BSTK RG21 3 F1
Lymington Cl KEMP RG22 54 C4
Lynch Hl WHCH RG28 47 F5
Lynch Hill Pk WHCH RG28 47 G5
The Lynch OVTN RG25 49 F2
WHCH RG28 47 G5
Lyndford Ter FLET GU13 33 F5
Lyndhurst Dr KEMP RG22 54 D4
Lynwood Dr AND SP10 56 C3
Lynwood Gdns HTWY RG27 30 C1
Lytton Rd BSTK RG21 3 H4

M

Mabbs La HTWY RG27 22 A5
Madeira Cl CHIN RG24 27 G3
Madeley Rd FLET GU13 45 H1
Madrid Rd AND SP10 57 G2
Magnolia Cl AND SP10 56 C4
Magnolia Wy FLET GU13 33 G5
Magnus Dr KEMP RG22 54 C3
Magpie Cl KEMP RG22 54 A2
Mahler Cl KEMP RG22 55 G2 1
Main Rd TADY RG26 5 G5
Majestic Rd KEMP RG22 54 B5
Majorca Av AND SP10 57 G2
Maldive Rd CHIN RG24 27 G3
Malham Gdns KEMP RG22 54 C5
Mallard Cl AND SP10 57 F1
KEMP RG22 54 A3
Mallards ALTN GU34 58 D2
Malshanger La DEAN RG23 35 H4
Malta Cl CHIN RG24 27 F3
Malthouse Cl FLET GU13 45 E2
Malthouse La TADY RG26 5 G5
Malthouse Ms ALTN GU34 59 G1 1
Maltings Cl ALTN GU34 58 D5
Malvern Cl KEMP RG22 37 F4
Manley James Cl ODIM RG29 43 G2 1
Manor Cl ALTN GU34 59 E1
KEMP RG22 54 B4
Manor Ct FLET GU13 45 G3
Manor La CHIN RG24 40 C1
Manor Rd ALTN GU34 59 E1
AND SP10 56 D2
CHIN RG24 26 B1
Manse La TADY RG26 5 G5
Mansfield Rd KEMP RG22 38 B5
Maple Cl ALTN GU34 58 D2 2
Maple Crs BSTK RG21 27 E5
Maple Gv TADY RG26 5 E3
Maplehurst Cha KEMP RG22 54 C4
Marchant Rd AND SP10 56 C4
March Cl AND SP10 57 F2
Margaret Rd KEMP RG22 38 A3
Marigold Cl KEMP RG22 54 B2
Mariners Cl TADY RG26 5 G5
Market Pl BSTK RG21 3 F5
Market Sq ALTN GU34 58 D4
Market St ALTN GU34 58 D4
Marlborough Gdns
DEAN RG23 36 A5 1
Marlborough St AND SP10 57 E3
Marlowe Cl CHIN RG24 27 F4
Marl's La CHIN RG24 19 E5
Marsden Ct WHCH RG28 48 D4 1
Marshall Gdns BSTK RG21 27 E5 1
Marshcourt CHIN RG24 28 A4
Martin Cl BSTK RG21 27 F5
Martins Cl ALTN GU34 59 E2
Martins Wd CHIN RG24 28 A1 3
Martin Wy AND SP10 57 F1 3
Mathias Wk KEMP RG22 55 E4
Matilda Dr KEMP RG22 54 C3 3
Matthews Wy DEAN RG23 53 F1
Mattock Wy CHIN RG24 28 A1
Maw Cl KEMP RG22 55 G2 2
Maybrook CHIN RG24 20 A5
May Cl CHIN RG24 40 D1
Mayfield Rdg DEAN RG23 54 C5
Mayflower Cl CHIN RG24 27 H2
Maynard's Wd CHIN RG24 27 H2

May Pl *BSTK* RG21 .... 3 F5
May Tree Rd *AND* SP10 .... 56 B2
Mccartney Wk *KEMP* RG22...... 54 D3
Mead Cl *AND* SP10 .... 56 D4
Meadowland *CHIN* RG24......... 27 H1
Meadow La *HTWY* RG27 .... 22 A3
Meadow Pound *WHCH* RG28 ... 47 G5 ▯
Meadowridge *KEMP* RG22....... 54 D5
Meadow Rd *BSTK* RG21........... 55 H1
Meadow Vw *FLET* GU13 .... 45 E2 ▯
   WHCH RG28 .... 47 E5
Meadow Wy *AND* SP10 .... 56 B3
Mead Rd *AND* SP10 .... 56 D4
The Mead *CHIN* RG24 .... 40 C1
Mede Cl *OVTN* RG25 .... 50 A3
Medina Gdns *DEAN* RG23 .... 53 E1 ▯
Medonte Cl *FLET* GU13 .... 33 H4 ▯
Medway Av *DEAN* RG23 .... 36 A5
Medway Gd *AND* SP10 .... 57 G1
   BSTK RG21 .... 3 K4
Melford Gdns *KEMP* RG22 ...... 37 F5
Memorial Rd *HTWY* RG27 .... 30 C2
Mendip Cl *KEMP* RG22 .... 37 F4
Meon Cl *TADY* RG26 .... 4 D2
Meon Rd *DEAN* RG23 .... 53 E1
Mercer Cl *KEMP* RG22 .... 37 H3
Merivale *FLET* GU13 .... 32 D4
Merlin Md *KEMP* RG22 .... 54 A4
Merriatt Cl *BSTK* RG21 .... 39 E5
Merrileas Gdns *KEMP* RG22 .... 54 B2
Merrydown La *CHIN* RG24 ...... 28 B2 ▯
Merryfield *CHIN* RG24 .... 27 H1
Merton Rd *BSTK* RG21 .... 2 B1
Micheldever Rd *AND* SP10 ...... 57 H4
Middle Md *HTWY* RG27 .... 30 C1 ▯
Middleton Gdns *BSTK* RG21 .... 27 E5 ▯
Midlane Cl *AND* SP10 .... 38 D5
Mildmay Ct *ODIM* RG29......... 43 G3
Milkingpen La *CHIN* RG24 ...... 28 C5
Millard Cl *BSTK* RG21 .... 26 C5
Millers Rd *TADY* RG26 .... 5 E3
Mill La *ALTN* GU34 .... 59 F3
   KSCL RG20 .... 8 B2
   ODIM RG29 .... 30 D5
Mill Rd *CHIN* RG24................ 25 H4
Millstream Cl *AND* SP10......... 56 D5
Millway Cl *AND* SP10 .... 56 C4
Millway Rd *AND* SP10............ 56 C3
Milton Av *AND* SP10 .... 56 B3
Milton Cl *CHIN* RG24 .... 27 F4
Minchens La *TADY* RG26 .... 15 H3
Minden Cl *FLET* GU13 .... 27 H2 ▯
Minley Gv *FARN* GU14 .... 33 H1 ▯
Minley Rd *FARN* GU14 .... 33 H1
Minstead Cl *TADY* RG26 .... 5 E5
Mitchell Av *HTWY* RG27 .... 22 A4
Mitchell Gdns *KEMP* RG22 ..... 54 D3 ▯
Moat Cl *TADY* RG26 .... 15 H2
Monachus La *HTWY* RG27 ...... 22 B2
Monarch Cl *KEMP* RG22 .... 54 B4
Mongers Piece *CHIN* RG24 ..... 20 B5
Monk Sherborne Rd *TADY* RG26 .. 16 C2
Monks Ri *FLET* GU13 .... 32 D3 ▯
Monks Wood Crs *TADY* RG26 ... 5 E4 ▯
Montague Pl *BSTK* RG21 .... 3 F7
Montrose Cl *FLET* GU13.......... 33 H4
Montserrat Pl *CHIN* RG24 ...... 27 F2 ▯
Montserrat Rd *CHIN* RG24 ...... 27 F2
Moore Cl *AND* SP10 .... 57 G2
   FLET GU13 .... 45 G2
Moore Rd *FLET* GU13............. 45 G2
Moorfoot Gdns *KEMP* RG22 .... 37 G4
Moorhams Av *KEMP* RG22 ...... 54 B4
The Moorings *BSTK* RG21 .... 3 K3
Moorlands Cl *FLET* GU13 .... 33 H4 ▯
Moor Vw *CHIN* RG24.............. 28 C5
Moreland Cl *ALTN* GU34......... 58 D5
Moreton Cl *FLET* GU13 .... 45 F3
Morgaston Rd *TADY* RG26 ...... 18 C2
Morley Rd *BSTK* RG21 .... 55 H1
Mornington Cl *TADY* RG26 ..... 4 A4
Morris St *HTWY* RG27 .... 30 A2
Morse Rd *KEMP* RG22 .... 38 B3
Mortimer Gdns *TADY* RG26 .... 5 E3
Mortimer La *BSTK* RG21 .... 2 D4
Moulshay La *HTWY* RG27 .... 20 D2
Mount Pleasant *HTWY* RG27 ... 22 B3
   TADY RG26 .... 4 B2
Mount Pleasant Rd *ALTN* GU34 ... 58 C5
The Mount *FLET* GU13 .... 33 G2
Mourne Cl *KEMP* RG22 .... 37 G3
Mozart Cl *KEMP* RG22 .... 55 F2
Mulberry Wy *CHIN* RG24 .... 28 A1
Mulfords Hl *TADY* RG26.......... 5 E3
Mull Cl *DEAN* RG23 .... 35 H5
Mullins Cl *BSTK* RG21 .... 27 E4
Munnings Cl *BSTK* RG21 .... 39 G4
Musgrave Cl *KEMP* RG22 .... 55 E2 ▯
Musgrove Gdns *ALTN* GU34 .... 58 C3
Musket Copse *CHIN* RG24 ...... 40 B1
Myland Cl *BSTK* RG21 .... 27 F4 ▯
Mylen Rd *AND* SP10 .... 56 C3

N

Napoleon Dr *DEAN* RG23.......... 25 H5
Nash Cl *BSTK* RG21 .... 27 F5
Neath Rd *BSTK* RG21 .... 3 J3
Nene Ct *AND* SP10 .... 57 G1 ▮▯
Nestor Cl *AND* SP10 .... 56 D2
Netherfield Cl *ALTN* GU34 ...... 58 C3
Netherhouse Moor *FLET* GU13 .. 32 D5 ▯
   FLET RG28 .... 44 D1
Neville Cl *AND* SP10 .... 57 F5
   BSTK RG21 .... 39 E5
New Barn Cl *FLET* GU13 .... 32 D5 ▯
New Barn La *ALTN* GU34 .... 58 D5
Newbury Rd *KSCL* RG20 .... 9 F3
   WHCH RG28 .... 47 G1
Newbury St *AND* SP10 .... 57 E3
   WHCH RG28 .... 47 F5
Newchurch Rd *TADY* RG26 ..... 4 D2
Newlands *FLET* GU13............. 45 G1
Newman La *ALTN* GU34 .... 59 F2
Newnham La *ODIM* RG29 .... 29 E4
Newnham Pk *HTWY* RG27 ...... 30 B2 ▯
New Odiham Rd *ALTN* GU34.... 58 B3
New Paddock Cl *ALTN* GU34 ... 59 G1
New Rd *BSTK* RG21 .... 3 F5
   FLET GU13 .... 45 H1
   HTWY RG27 .... 22 A3
   HTWY RG27 .... 30 C1
   ODIM RG29 .... 43 E1
   TADY RG26 .... 4 D4
   TADY RG26 .... 13 H3
New St *AND* SP10 .... 57 F3
   BSTK RG21 .... 2 E5
Newtown *TADY* RG26 .... 4 D2
Newtown Cl *AND* SP10 .... 56 C4 ▯
Nightingale Gdns *CHIN* RG24 .. 25 H4
   HTWY RG27 .... 30 C1
Nightingale Ri *OVTN* RG25 ..... 50 A3
Norden Cl *BSTK* RG21 .... 3 F1
Normandy St *ALTN* GU34 .... 58 D3
Normanton Rd *BSTK* RG21 ..... 27 E4 ▯
   BSTK RG21 .... 27 E4 ▯
Norn Hi *BSTK* RG21 .... 3 H1
Norn Hill Cl *BSTK* RG21 .... 3 H1
Northanger Cl *ALTN* GU34...... 58 C3
Northern Av *AND* SP10 .... 57 F3
Northfield Cl *FLET* GU13 .... 45 H1 ▯
Northfield Rd *FLET* GU13 .... 45 H1
North St *KSCL* RG20 .... 9 G4
North View Rd *TADY* RG26 ..... 5 E4
North Warnborough St
   ODIM RG29 .... 42 D2
Norton Ride *CHIN* RG24.......... 28 A5
Novello Cl *KEMP* RG22 .... 55 F5
Nursery Cl *CHIN* RG24 .... 28 B1 ▯
Nursery Rd *ALTN* GU34 .... 59 E3

O

Oak Bank *AND* SP10............... 57 E5
Oak Cl *DEAN* RG23 .... 53 E1
   OVTN RG25 .... 49 H4
Oakdene *ALTN* GU34 .... 58 C2
Oaken Copse *FLET* GU13 .... 45 H3
Oakfield Rd *TADY* RG26 .... 5 H2
Oakfields Cl *KSCL* RG20 .... 8 A2
Oak Hanger Cl *HTWY* RG27 .... 30 D1 ▯
Oakland Cl *WHCH* RG28 .... 47 F5
Oaklands Wy *DEAN* RG23 .... 37 H1
Oakley Dr *FLET* GU13 .... 33 G4
Oakley La *DEAN* RG23 .... 36 A5
Oakmead *TADY* RG26 .... 15 H2
Oakridge Rd *BSTK* RG21 .... 26 D5
The Oaks *FLET* GU13 .... 32 D3
   TADY RG26 .... 4 D3
Oak Tree Cl *TADY* RG26 .... 5 E2 ▯
Oakwood *CHIN* RG24 .... 28 A1
   FLET GU13 .... 45 G3
Oban Cl *DEAN* RG23 .... 35 H5
O'bee Gdns *TADY* RG26 .... 4 B2
Ochil Cl *KEMP* RG22 .... 37 G4
Octavian Cl *KEMP* RG22 .... 54 C3
Odette Gdns *TADY* RG26 .... 5 E2
Old Acre Rd *ALTN* GU34 .... 59 E4
Oldberg Gdns *KEMP* RG22 ..... 55 G2 ▯
Old Common Rd *BSTK* RG21 ... 3 J6
Old Cove Rd *FARN* GU14 .... 33 H1
Old Down Cl *KEMP* RG22 .... 54 B1
Old Down Rd *AND* SP10 .... 56 D2
Oldfield Vw *HTWY* RG27 .... 22 A4 ▯
Old Kempshott La *KEMP* RG22 ... 37 F4
Old Odiham Rd *ALTN* GU34 .... 58 D3
Old Pumphouse Cl *FLET* GU13 ... 33 H2
Old Reading Rd *BSTK* RG21 .... 3 G2
Old School Cl *FLET* GU13 .... 33 G3 ▯
   HTWY RG27 .... 22 B3 ▯
Old School Rd *HTWY* RG27 ..... 30 A2
Old Vyne La *TADY* RG26 .... 12 C5

Old Winton Rd *AND* SP10 .... 57 F4
Old Worting Rd *KEMP* RG22 .... 37 H3
Oliver Ri *ALTN* GU34 .... 58 D3
Oliver's Wk *CHIN* RG24 .... 28 A5
Omega *ALTN* GU34 .... 59 F4
Onslow Cl *CHIN* RG24 .... 59 E3
Orchard La *ALTN* GU34 .... 59 E5
Orchard Rd *AND* SP10 .... 57 H3
The Orchard *OVTN* RG25 .... 49 H2
   TADY RG26 .... 5 G3
Orkney Cl *ALTN* GU34 .... 27 G3
   BSTK RG21 .... 3 K2
Osborne Cl *ALTN* GU34 .... 58 B4
Osborne Dr *FLET* GU13 .... 33 H5
Osborne Rd *AND* SP10............ 56 D4
Osborn Wy *HTWY* RG27 .... 30 D2
Osprey Cl *KEMP* RG22 .... 54 A1
Osprey Rd *KEMP* RG22 .... 54 A1
Otterbourne Crs *TADY* RG26 ... 5 E5
Ouse Ct *AND* SP10 .... 57 G1
Oyster Cl *KEMP* RG22 .... 54 B5

P

Packenham Rd *BSTK* RG21....... 2 B6
Pack La *DEAN* RG23 .... 36 A4
   KEMP RG22 .... 37 F5
Paddock Ct *HTWY* RG27 .... 22 A4 ▯
Paddockfields *CHIN* RG24 .... 28 C5
Paddock Rd *KEMP* RG22 .... 38 A4
The Paddock *HTWY* RG27 .... 22 B2
   KSCL RG20 .... 9 F4
Padwick Cl *BSTK* RG21........... 2 C6
Painters Pightle *HTWY* RG27 ... 30 B1
Palace Ga *ODIM* RG29 .... 43 F2
Pale La *HTWY* RG27 .... 23 F5
Palmer Cl *BSTK* RG21 .... 27 H4
Palmer Dr *AND* SP10 .... 57 H3 ▯
Pamber Heath Rd *TADY* RG26 .. 5 G3
Pamber Rd *THLE* RG7 .... 6 B2
Pantile Dr *HTWY* RG27 .... 31 E1
Papermakers *OVTN* RG25 ...... 50 A3
Paper Mill La *ALTN* GU34 .... 59 E3
The Parade *TADY* RG26 .... 5 E2 ▯
Pardown *DEAN* RG23............. 53 E3
Park Av *CHIN* RG24 .... 40 C2
Park Cl *DEAN* RG23 .... 35 H5
Park Close Rd *ALTN* GU34 ...... 59 E2
Park Gdns *BSTK* RG21 .... 3 H7
Park Hl *FLET* GU13 .... 45 F4
Park La *CHIN* RG24 .... 40 C2
Park Pl *FLET* GU13 .... 45 F2
Parkside Rd *BSTK* RG21 .... 3 G7
Parkview Cl *AND* SP10 .... 56 C1
Parkwood Cl *CHIN* RG24 .... 20 A5 ▯
Parsons Cl *FLET* GU13 .... 45 F2
Partridge Gn *ALTN* GU34 .... 58 D2
Paterson Cl *KEMP* RG22 .... 54 D5
Paulet Pl *CHIN* RG24 .... 40 C1
Pawmers Md *FLET* GU13 .... 44 D4
Paxton Cl *KEMP* RG22 .... 54 C5 ▯
Pearman Dr *AND* SP10 .... 57 H3
Pear Tree Av *FLET* GU13 .... 33 F2 ▯
Peat Moor Cl *FLET* GU13 .... 33 E2 ▯
Peatmoor Cl *FLET* GU13 .... 33 E2
Peel Ct *HTWY* RG27 .... 22 A5 ▯
Peel Gdns *KSCL* RG20 .... 9 F3
Pelham Cl *CHIN* RG24 .... 40 C2
Pelican Rd *KEMP* RG22 .... 53 H5
Pelican Rd *TADY* RG26 .... 5 F2
Pelton Rd *BSTK* RG21 .... 2 B2
Pembroke Rd *DEAN* RG23 ...... 37 G2 ▯
Pemerton Rd *BSTK* RG21 .... 27 F5
Pen Cl *AND* SP10 .... 57 G3
Pendennis Cl *DEAN* RG23 ...... 37 G1
Pennine Wy *KEMP* RG22 .... 37 G4
Penny's Hatch *KSCL* RG20 ..... 9 H4
Penrith Rd *BSTK* RG21 .... 2 C5
Pentland Cl *KEMP* RG22 .... 37 G4
Perry Dr *FLET* GU13 .... 32 D3
Pershore Rd *CHIN* RG24 .... 27 E3
Petersfield Cl *CHIN* RG24 .... 20 C5 ▯
Petrel Cft *KEMP* RG22 .... 54 B2 ▯
Petty's Brook Rd *CHIN* RG24 ... 20 A5
Petunia Cl *KEMP* RG22 .... 54 B2
Petworth Cl *KEMP* RG22 .... 54 C4 ▯
Pheaben's Fld *TADY* RG26 ...... 15 H3 ▯
Pheasant Cl *KEMP* RG22 .... 54 A2
Pheasant Copse *FLET* GU13 ... 32 D2
Pheby Rd *KEMP* RG22 .... 38 A5
Phoenix Ct *KSCL* RG20 .... 9 G4
Phoenix Park Ter *BSTK* RG21 .. 2 E2
Pilcot Rd *HTWY* RG27 .... 44 B1
Pilgrims Wy *AND* SP10 .... 57 G2
Pimpernel Wy *CHIN* RG24 ...... 28 A5
Pine Cv *FLET* GU13 .... 45 H2
Pinehurst *TADY* RG26 .... 5 E3
Pines Rd *FLET* GU13 .... 33 F2
The Pines *AND* SP10.............. 56 D3
Pinewood Cl *TADY* RG26 .... 4 A2

Pinewood Hl *FLET* GU13 .... 33 G2
Pinkerton Rd *KEMP* RG22 .... 37 H5
Pinks La *TADY* RG26 .... 4 B2
Pinnell Cl *KEMP* RG22 .... 54 B1
Pintail Cl *KEMP* RG22 .... 54 A3 ▯
Pipers Cft *FLET* GU13 .... 45 G3 ▯
Pitcairn Cl *CHIN* RG24 .... 27 F2
Pither Rd *ODIM* RG29 .... 43 E5
Pitman Cl *KEMP* RG22 .... 54 D3
Pittard Rd *BSTK* RG21 .... 2 B7
Pitts La *AND* SP10................. 57 E5
Plantation Rd *AND* SP10 .... 56 C4
   TADY RG26 .... 4 B1
Pleasant Hl *TADY* RG26 .... 5 E3
Plover Cl *AND* SP10 .... 57 F1 ▯
   KEMP RG22 .... 54 B1
Plovers Wy *ALTN* GU34 .... 59 E1
Plumpton Wy *ALTN* GU34 ...... 58 D5 ▯
Poland La *ODIM* RG29 .... 31 G4
Polkerris Wy *FLET* GU13......... 45 H3 ▯
Polmear Cl *FLET* GU13 .... 45 H3
Pond Cl *OVTN* RG25 .... 49 H4
Pond Rd *HTWY* RG27 .... 22 A2
Poors Farm Rd *CHIN* RG24 ..... 29 F4
Popes Hl *KSCL* RG20 .... 9 F4
Poplar Cl *TADY* RG26 .... 4 A3
Popley Wy *CHIN* RG24 .... 27 F5
Poppy Flds *CHIN* RG24 .... 28 B4
Portacre Ri *BSTK* RG21 .... 2 A7
Porter Cl *ODIM* RG29 .... 43 E5 ▯
Porter Rd *KEMP* RG22 .... 55 G1
Portiswood Cl *TADY* RG26 ...... 5 G3 ▯
Portland Dr *FLET* GU13.......... 45 F3
Portland Gv *AND* SP10 .... 57 E3 ▯
Portway *TADY* RG26 .... 4 A2
Portway Cl *AND* SP10 .... 56 B3
Portway Pl *DEAN* RG23 .... 37 G2
Portway Rd *DEAN* RG23 .... 37 G2
Potbridge Rd *ODIM* RG29 ...... 31 H2
Pot La *CHIN* RG24 .... 29 G4
Poultons Cl *OVTN* RG25 .... 49 H4
Poultons Rd *OVTN* RG25 .... 49 H4
Pound Cl *TADY* RG26 .... 15 H3
Pound Ga *ALTN* GU34 .... 59 E2 ▯
Pound Meadow *HTWY* RG27 ... 21 F1
Pound Rd *OVTN* RG25 .... 50 A3
Poveys Md *KSCL* RG20 .... 9 H4
Poynings Crs *BSTK* RG21 .... 39 F5
Poynters Cl *AND* SP10 .... 56 D1
Poyntz Rd *OVTN* RG25 .... 49 H2
Priestley Rd *CHIN* RG24 .... 26 B5
Primrose Dr *HTWY* RG27 .... 22 B2
Primrose Gdns *KEMP* RG22 .... 54 C5
Princes' Crs *KEMP* RG22 .... 38 B4
Princess Dr *ALTN* GU34 .... 58 B4
Priors Cl *KSCL* RG20 .... 9 G4 ▯
Priors Keep *FLET* GU13 .... 33 H4
Priors Rd *TADY* RG26 .... 4 D2
Priory Cl *FLET* GU13 .... 32 D4
Priory Gdns *CHIN* RG24 .... 28 C5
Priory La *HTWY* RG27 .... 22 A5
   WHCH RG28 .... 48 B3
Privett Cl *CHIN* RG24 .... 28 B4
Provident Wy *BSTK* RG21 ...... 2 E5
Puffin Cl *KEMP* RG22 .... 54 A4
Purbrook Rd *TADY* RG26........ 4 D3
Purcell Cl *KEMP* RG22 .... 55 G1
Puttenham Rd *CHIN* RG24 ..... 28 B1
Pyotts Copse *CHIN* RG24 .... 28 B3
Pyotts Ct *CHIN* RG24 .... 28 B3
Pyotts Hl *CHIN* RG24 .... 28 B3

Q

Queen Mary Av *BSTK* RG21..... 3 F1
Queen Mary Cl *FLET* GU13 ..... 33 F2
Queens Av *AND* SP10 .... 56 D3
Queens Rd *ALTN* GU34 .... 58 C4
   BSTK RG21 .... 3 B5
   FLET GU13 .... 33 G5
   KSCL RG20 .... 9 H4
   ODIM RG29 .... 43 E2 ▯
Quilter Rd *KEMP* RG22 .... 54 D2
Quince Tree Wy *HTWY* RG27 ... 30 D1

R

Rack Cl *AND* SP10 .... 57 F3
Rack Close Rd *ALTN* GU34 ...... 58 C4
Radford Gdns *BSTK* RG21 .... 38 C5
Rainbow Cl *CHIN* RG24 .... 40 D2
Rainham Cl *KEMP* RG22 .... 54 A3
Ramparts *AND* SP10 .... 56 C5
The Ramparts *AND* SP10 .... 56 C5
Rampton's Meadow *TADY* RG26 .. 5 C4
Ramsdell Cl *TADY* RG26 .... 5 C4
Ramsdell Rd *TADY* RG26......... 10 D5
   TADY RG26 .... 13 C5
Raphael Cl *BSTK* RG21 .... 3 K7
Ravel Cl *KEMP* RG22 .... 55 F1

Raven Rd *HTWY* RG27 .... 30 C1
Ravens Cft *HTWY* RG27 .... 31 E1 🔲
Raven Sq *ALTN* GU34 .... 58 D1
Rawlings Rd *HTWY* RG27 .... 30 D2
Rayleigh Rd *BSTK* RG21 .... 2 D4
Reading Rd *CHIN* RG24 .... 27 H2
    HTWY RG27 .... 21 E1
Reading Rd North *FLET* GU13 .... 32 D2
Reading Rd South *FLET* GU13 .... 33 C5
Rebecca Cl *FLET* GU13 .... 45 E4
Recreation Rd *AND* SP10 .... 57 F3 🔲
    ODIM RG29 .... 43 E3
Rectory Cl *TADY* RG26 .... 5 F5
Rectory Rd *DEAN* RG23 .... 52 B1
    HTWY RG27 .... 30 C2
Redbridge Dr *AND* SP10 .... 56 D5
Redbridge La *CHIN* RG24 .... 39 H2
Red Lion La *BSTK* RG21 .... 3 E5
    OVTN RG25 .... 49 H2
Redon Wy *AND* SP10 .... 56 D2
Redwing Cl *KEMP* RG22 .... 54 A3
Redwoods Wy *FLET* GU13 .... 45 H5
Regent Cl *FLET* GU13 .... 33 G4
Regent St *FLET* GU13 .... 33 G4
Rembrandt Cl *BSTK* RG21 .... 3 K7
Rememberance Gdns
    CHIN RG24 .... 28 A2 🔲
Renoir Cl *BSTK* RG21 .... 39 C4
Renown Wy *CHIN* RG24 .... 20 A5 🔲
Restormel Cl *DEAN* RG23 .... 37 G1
Reuben's Crs *TADY* RG26 .... 5 E4
Reynards Cl *TADY* RG26 .... 5 E3
Reynolds Cl *BSTK* RG21 .... 3 K6
Reyntiens Vw *ODIM* RG29 .... 43 G2 🔲
Ribble Ct *AND* SP10 .... 57 G1
Ribble Wy *BSTK* RG21 .... 3 J4
Richard Cl *FLET* GU13 .... 33 E5
Richmond Cl *FLET* GU13 .... 45 F1
Richmond Rd *BSTK* RG21 .... 2 D1
Ridge Cl *KEMP* RG22 .... 54 D5
The Ridgeway *ALTN* GU34 .... 58 D5
Ridley Cl *FLET* GU13 .... 33 F5
Riley La *CHIN* RG24 .... 26 C5
Rimes's La *TADY* RG26 .... 4 C5
Ringshall Gdns *TADY* RG26 .... 15 H3
Ringway East *CHIN* RG24 .... 27 G5
Ringway North *CHIN* RG24 .... 26 B5
Ringway South *BSTK* RG21 .... 3 J7
    KEMP RG22 .... 38 B3
River Pde *AND* SP10 .... 57 G1
Riverside Cl *CHIN* RG24 .... 28 C5
    OVTN RG25 .... 50 A2
River Wy *AND* SP10 .... 57 F1
Robert Mays Rd *ODIM* RG29 .... 43 E3 🔲
Robin Cl *ALTN* GU34 .... 59 E1
    KEMP RG22 .... 54 B2
Robin Wy *AND* SP10 .... 57 F1
Rochester Cl *KEMP* RG22 .... 54 C2 🔲
Rochester Gv *FLET* GU13 .... 33 F4
Rochford Rd *BSTK* RG21 .... 2 C4
Roding Cl *BSTK* RG21 .... 3 J4
Roentgen Rd *CHIN* RG24 .... 27 H5
Rogers Ct *ALTN* GU34 .... 58 D3
Roman Rd *DEAN* RG23 .... 37 G2
Romans Fld *THLE* RG7 .... 6 C3 🔲
Romans Ga *THLE* RG7 .... 6 A2
Roman Wy *DEAN* RG23 .... 37 G2
Romsey Cl *CHIN* RG24 .... 26 D3
The Rookery *WHCH* RG28 .... 47 F5 🔲
Rooksbury Rd *AND* SP10 .... 56 C5
Rooksdown Av *CHIN* RG24 .... 25 H4
Rooksdown La *CHIN* RG24 .... 25 H3
Rookswood *ALTN* GU34 .... 58 D2
Rookswood Cl *HTWY* RG27 .... 30 D1 🔲
Ropley Cl *TADY* RG26 .... 4 D4
Roseberry Cl *KEMP* RG22 .... 54 C5
Rose Cl *KEMP* RG22 .... 54 C2
Rosedene Gdns *FLET* GU13 .... 33 F2
Rosehip Cl *CHIN* RG24 .... 20 A5
Rose Hodson Pl *DEAN* RG23 .... 25 H5
Rosemary Dr *TADY* RG26 .... 5 E5
Rose Wk *FLET* GU13 .... 33 F2
Ross Cl *BSTK* RG21 .... 38 D5 🔲
Rossini Cl *KEMP* RG22 .... 55 F2
Rothay Cl *BSTK* RG21 .... 3 J4
Rotherwick Rd *TADY* RG26 .... 5 E4
Rotten Hl *OVTN* RG25 .... 49 F4
Roundmead Rd *BSTK* RG21 .... 2 C5
Roundway Ct *AND* SP10 .... 56 C5
Rounton Rd *FLET* GU13 .... 45 G2
Rowan Dl *FLET* GU13 .... 45 F2
Rowan Rd *TADY* RG26 .... 4 D4
Royal Cl *DEAN* RG23 .... 54 B5
Rubens Cl *BSTK* RG21 .... 39 C5
Rufford Cl *FLET* GU13 .... 45 G1
The Rushes *BSTK* RG21 .... 3 K4
Rushmoor Cl *FLET* GU13 .... 45 G3
Russell Rd *BSTK* RG21 .... 3 F7
Russett Rd *ALTN* GU34 .... 59 E4
Russetts Dr *FLET* GU13 .... 33 G4
Rustic Gln *FLET* GU13 .... 45 F2
Rutherford Rd *CHIN* RG24 .... 27 G4

Rydal Dr *FLET* GU13 .... 45 E2
Ryebeck Rd *FLET* GU13 .... 45 G2
Rye Cft *FLET* GU13 .... 45 E3
Ryelaw Rd *FLET* GU13 .... 45 G2

S

Saffron Cl *CHIN* RG24 .... 20 A5
Sainfoin La *CHIN* RG23 .... 53 E2
Sainsbury Cl *AND* SP10 .... 56 D5
St Andrew's Rd *KEMP* RG22 .... 38 A4
St Ann's Cl *AND* SP10 .... 57 E4 🔲
St Christophers Cl *KEMP* RG22 .... 37 H4 🔲
St Davids Cl *ODIM* RG29 .... 43 E3 🔲
St David's Rd *KEMP* RG22 .... 38 B4
St Gabriels Lea *CHIN* RG24 .... 28 B1
St Hubert Rd *AND* SP10 .... 56 C4
St James Rd *FLET* GU13 .... 33 F4
St Johns Cl *HTWY* RG27 .... 30 D1 🔲
St John's Piece *DEAN* RG23 .... 53 E2
St John's Rd *AND* SP10 .... 36 A5
    DEAN RG23 .... 36 A5
    HTWY RG27 .... 22 B4
St Joseph's Crs *CHIN* RG24 .... 28 A2 🔲
St Lawrence Rd *ALTN* GU34 .... 58 B5
St Leonard's Av *CHIN* RG24 .... 28 B1
St Marys Cl *ALTN* GU34 .... 58 D5
St Mary's Ct *BSTK* RG21 .... 3 C4
St Mary's Rd *HTWY* RG27 .... 22 A4
    KSCL RG20 .... 9 G4
St Michael's Rd *KEMP* RG22 .... 37 H4
St Nicholas Cl *FLET* GU13 .... 33 F3
St Nicholas Ct *KEMP* RG22 .... 38 B4
St Patrick's Rd *KEMP* RG22 .... 38 B4
St Paul's Rd *KEMP* RG22 .... 38 A4
St Peter's Rd *KEMP* RG22 .... 38 B4
St Thomas' Cl *BSTK* RG21 .... 27 E5 🔲
Salisbury Cl *ALTN* GU34 .... 59 E5
    ODIM RG29 .... 43 E3 🔲
Salisbury Gdns *KEMP* RG22 .... 37 H3
Salisbury Rd *AND* SP10 .... 56 C5
Salmons Rd *ODIM* RG29 .... 43 E3
Salters Heath Rd *TADY* RG26 .... 17 G3
Sandbanks Dr *KEMP* RG22 .... 54 C3 🔲
Sandford Cl *KSCL* RG20 .... 10 A4
Sandford Rd *BSTK* RG21 .... 4 D3
Sandown Cl *ALTN* GU34 .... 59 E5 🔲
Sandpiper Wy *KEMP* RG22 .... 54 A3
Sandringham Cl *ALTN* GU34 .... 58 B4 🔲
Sandy La *FLET* GU13 .... 45 G3
    HTWY RG27 .... 22 B4
    TADY RG26 .... 5 G3
Sandys Cl *KEMP* RG22 .... 38 B4
Sandys Rd *KEMP* RG22 .... 38 B3
Saor Ms *AND* SP10 .... 56 D3 🔲
Sapley La *OVTN* RG25 .... 49 H3
Sarisbury Cl *TADY* RG26 .... 4 D5
Sarum Hl *BSTK* RG21 .... 2 D5
Sarum Rd *TADY* RG26 .... 4 D2
Savoy Cl *AND* SP10 .... 57 F4
Saxon Wy *CHIN* RG24 .... 28 A5
Scarlatti Rd *KEMP* RG22 .... 54 F2
School La *THLE* RG7 .... 6 C2
Schroeder Cl *BSTK* RG21 .... 38 D5
Schubert Rd *KEMP* RG22 .... 55 F2
Scotney Rd *BSTK* RG21 .... 27 E5
Scures Rd *HTWY* RG27 .... 30 B1
Seagull Cl *KEMP* RG22 .... 54 A2 🔲
Seal Rd *BSTK* RG21 .... 3 F4
Searing Wy *TADY* RG26 .... 4 D2
Second Av *THLE* RG7 .... 6 F1
Selborne Cl *HTWY* RG27 .... 30 D1
Seton Dr *HTWY* RG27 .... 30 B2 🔲
The Severals *CHIN* RG24 .... 26 B1
Severn Gdns *DEAN* RG23 .... 53 E1
Severn Wy *BSTK* RG21 .... 3 K4
Seville Crs *AND* SP10 .... 57 G2
Seymour Rd *KEMP* RG22 .... 37 H5
Shakespeare Av *AND* SP10 .... 56 B2
Shakespeare Rd *CHIN* RG24 .... 27 F4
Shaldon Wy *FLET* GU13 .... 32 D4 🔲
Shaw Cl *AND* SP10 .... 56 A3
Shaw Cl *TADY* RG26 .... 4 C5
Shaw Pightle *HTWY* RG27 .... 30 B1 🔲
Sheep Fair Cl *AND* SP10 .... 57 G3
Sheepwash La *TADY* RG26 .... 16 C3
Sheldon's La *HTWY* RG27 .... 30 C1
Sheldon's Rd *HTWY* RG27 .... 30 C1
Shelley Cl *CHIN* RG24 .... 27 F4
    FLET GU13 .... 33 G4
Shepherds Rw *AND* SP10 .... 57 G4
Shepherds Spring La *AND* SP10 .... 57 E3
Sheppard Rd *BSTK* RG21 .... 38 D5
Sheraton Av *KEMP* RG22 .... 54 D4
Sherborne Rd *BSTK* RG21 .... 26 C2
    CHIN RG24 .... 26 C2
Sheridan Crs *TADY* RG26 .... 5 E4
Sherwood Cl *KEMP* RG22 .... 54 D4
Shetland Rd *CHIN* RG24 .... 27 F2
Shipton Wy *KEMP* RG22 .... 37 H5
Shyshack La *TADY* RG26 .... 4 B2

Sian Cl *FLET* GU13 .... 45 H2
Sibelius Cl *KEMP* RG22 .... 55 F3
Sidlaw Cl *KEMP* RG22 .... 37 F4 🔲
Sidmouth Rd *AND* SP10 .... 57 G3
Silchester Cl *AND* SP10 .... 56 C1
    TADY RG26 .... 14 B1
    TADY RG26 .... 15 E3
Silk Mill La *OVTN* RG25 .... 49 G2
Silkweavers Rd *AND* SP10 .... 57 F3 🔲
Silver Birch Cl *FLET* GU13 .... 45 F2
Silver Birch Rd *AND* SP10 .... 56 C2 🔲
Silverdale *FLET* GU13 .... 45 G1
Silverdale Rd *TADY* RG26 .... 4 D2
Silver Park Cl *FLET* GU13 .... 45 H1
Silvester Cl *CHIN* RG24 .... 27 F5
Silvester Wy *FLET* GU13 .... 45 E3
Simons Rd *CHIN* RG24 .... 27 H2
Skates La *TADY* RG26 .... 13 G1
Skippetts La East *BSTK* RG21 .... 39 F5
Skippetts La West *BSTK* RG21 .... 39 E5
Skylark Ri *WHCH* RG28 .... 47 E4
Smallfield Dr *HTWY* RG27 .... 31 E1
Snowdrop Cl *KEMP* RG22 .... 54 B2 🔲
Soke Rd *THLE* RG7 .... 6 A1
Solby's Rd *BSTK* RG21 .... 2 C3
Solent Dr *KEMP* RG22 .... 54 C3
Sonning Cl *KEMP* RG22 .... 54 C3
Soper Gv *BSTK* RG21 .... 2 E1
Sorrell's Cl *CHIN* RG24 .... 28 A1
Southby Dr *FLET* GU13 .... 33 H3
Southdown Rd *TADY* RG26 .... 4 D2
South End Rd *AND* SP10 .... 57 F5
Southend Rd *BSTK* RG21 .... 2 C2
Southern Haye *HTWY* RG27 .... 22 A4
Southern Rd *BSTK* RG21 .... 2 C4
South Ham Rd *KEMP* RG22 .... 38 B3
Southington Cl *OVTN* RG25 .... 49 F2
Southington La *OVTN* RG25 .... 49 G2
Southlands *CHIN* RG24 .... 27 H1 🔲
South Rdg *ODIM* RG29 .... 43 G3
South Rd *KSCL* RG20 .... 9 H4
South St *AND* SP10 .... 57 E5
South View Cottages
    WHCH RG28 .... 48 B3
South View Gdns *AND* SP10 .... 57 F4
Southview Ri *ALTN* GU34 .... 58 C2 🔲
Speckled Wood Rd *CHIN* RG24 .... 27 E3
Spencer Cl *TADY* RG26 .... 5 H2 🔲
Spenser Cl *ALTN* GU34 .... 59 E2
Sperrin Cl *KEMP* RG22 .... 37 G4
Spicers *ALTN* GU34 .... 59 E4
Spiers Cl *TADY* RG26 .... 5 G5
The Spinney *FLET* GU13 .... 32 D4 🔲
Spitalfields Rd *ALTN* GU34 .... 58 D5
Spitalhatch *ALTN* GU34 .... 59 F4
Spring Cl *CHIN* RG24 .... 26 A1
Springfield *DEAN* RG23 .... 36 A5
Springfield Av *HTWY* RG27 .... 22 A2
Springfield Cl *AND* SP10 .... 57 H3
Springfield La *FLET* GU13 .... 33 E5
Springfield Rd *TADY* RG26 .... 5 H2
Spring Ms *AND* SP10 .... 57 F2 🔲
Springwell La *HTWY* RG27 .... 22 B1
Spring Woods *FLET* GU13 .... 33 H5
Spruce Cl *AND* SP10 .... 56 A4 🔲
Stable Cl *HTWY* RG27 .... 30 B2
Stag Hl *KEMP* RG22 .... 38 A5
Stanfield *TADY* RG26 .... 5 E3
Stanford Rd *KEMP* RG22 .... 38 B4
Stanton Dr *FLET* GU13 .... 33 E4
Starling Cl *KEMP* RG22 .... 54 A2
Station Ap *AND* SP10 .... 56 D3
Station Rd *ALTN* GU34 .... 59 E3
    DEAN RG23 .... 30 C1
    HTWY RG27 .... 30 C1
    OVTN RG25 .... 49 G2
    WHCH RG28 .... 47 F4
Steeple Dr *ALTN* GU34 .... 58 D3
Stephenson Cl *AND* SP10 .... 56 A2
Stephens Rd *TADY* RG26 .... 5 F5
Sterling Pk *AND* SP10 .... 56 A2
Stiles Dr *AND* SP10 .... 57 E3
Stillions Cl *ALTN* GU34 .... 59 E4
Stockbridge Cl *CHIN* RG24 .... 26 D4
Stocker Cl *BSTK* RG21 .... 38 D5
Stockton Av *FLET* GU13 .... 33 F2
Stockton Pk *FLET* GU13 .... 33 F2
Stone Cl *AND* SP10 .... 56 C4
Stourhead Cl *AND* SP10 .... 56 C4
Stour Rd *DEAN* RG23 .... 53 E1
Stratfield Av *TADY* RG26 .... 5 E4
Stratfield Rd *BSTK* RG21 .... 27 E4 🔲
Stratton Rd *BSTK* RG21 .... 38 C5
Strauss Rd *KEMP* RG22 .... 54 D2
Stravinsky Rd *KEMP* RG22 .... 55 G2
Streamside *FLET* GU13 .... 33 G4 🔲
Street End *HTWY* RG27 .... 23 F5
The Street *CHIN* RG24 .... 40 B1
    FLET GU13 .... 44 D2
    ODIM RG29 .... 42 B2
    TADY RG26 .... 15 G4
Strokins Rd *KSCL* RG20 .... 9 G3
Stroud Cl *CHIN* RG24 .... 27 H2

Stroud La *HTWY* RG27 .... 44 C2
Stroudley Rd *CHIN* RG24 .... 27 H5
Stubbs Court Ct *AND* SP10 .... 56 D2
Stubbs Rd *BSTK* RG21 .... 39 F5
Stukeley Rd *BSTK* RG21 .... 2 B6
Suffolk Rd *AND* SP10 .... 56 D1
Sullivan Rd *KEMP* RG22 .... 55 F1
Summer Down La *DEAN* RG23 .... 35 F3
Summerfields *CHIN* RG24 .... 20 B5 🔲
Sunflower Cl *KEMP* RG22 .... 54 B3 🔲
Sunny Md *DEAN* RG23 .... 53 E2
Sunnyside *FLET* GU13 .... 33 E2
Sunnyside Cl *AND* SP10 .... 56 D5
Sutton Rd *BSTK* RG21 .... 27 E5
Swains Cl *TADY* RG26 .... 5 E3
Swains Rd *TADY* RG26 .... 5 E3
Swallow Cl *ALTN* GU34 .... 59 E1
    KEMP RG22 .... 54 A2
Swallowfields *AND* SP10 .... 57 F1
Swan Ct *HTWY* RG27 .... 22 B5 🔲
Swan Ms *ODIM* RG29 .... 43 E1 🔲
Swan St *KSCL* RG20 .... 9 G5
Swan Wy *FLET* GU13 .... 32 D5
Swedish Houses *TADY* RG26 .... 5 F4
Swift Cl *AND* SP10 .... 57 F1
Swing Swang La *CHIN* RG24 .... 27 H5
Sycamore Crs *FLET* GU13 .... 45 E1
Sycamore Wy *DEAN* RG23 .... 26 A5
Sylvan Wy *FLET* GU13 .... 45 F2
Sympson Rd *TADY* RG26 .... 5 G2

T

Tadley Common Rd *TADY* RG26 .... 5 F2
Tadley Hl *TADY* RG26 .... 5 F4
Tallis Gdns *KEMP* RG22 .... 55 F1
Talmey Cl *CHIN* RG24 .... 27 H1
Tamar Dr *DEAN* RG23 .... 53 E1
Tamarisk Cl *KEMP* RG22 .... 54 D5 🔲
Tangway *CHIN* RG24 .... 20 A5
Tanhouse La *ALTN* GU34 .... 58 C4
Tanners Wy *DEAN* RG23 .... 36 A5
Tasmania Cl *CHIN* RG24 .... 27 F2 🔲
Taverner Cl *BSTK* RG21 .... 27 G5
Tavistock Rd *FLET* GU13 .... 32 D4 🔲
Teal Crs *KEMP* RG22 .... 54 A3
Tennyson Wy *KEMP* RG22 .... 38 B4 🔲
Test Wy *BSTK* RG21 .... 3 J4
Tewkesbury Cl *CHIN* RG24 .... 27 E3
Thames Ct *AND* SP10 .... 57 H1 🔲
    BSTK RG21 .... 3 J3
Thirlmere Crs *FLET* GU13 .... 45 E2 🔲
Thistledown Cl *AND* SP10 .... 56 C2 🔲
Thorneley Rd *KSCL* RG20 .... 9 G4 🔲
Thornhill Wy *CHIN* RG24 .... 20 A5
Thornton End *ALTN* GU34 .... 59 G1
Thorpe Gdns *ALTN* GU34 .... 58 B3
Three Castles Pth *ODIM* RG29 .... 42 B3
Thumwood *CHIN* RG24 .... 28 A1 🔲
Thurston Pl *BSTK* RG21 .... 55 G1
Thyme Cl *CHIN* RG24 .... 20 B5
Tiberius Cl *DEAN* RG23 .... 25 H5
Tilney Cl *ALTN* GU34 .... 58 C3
Timberlake Rd *BSTK* RG21 .... 2 E4
Tintagel Cl *DEAN* RG23 .... 37 H3
Tintern Cl *CHIN* RG24 .... 26 C4
Tippet Gdns *KEMP* RG22 .... 55 G2
Titchfield Cl *TADY* RG26 .... 5 F4 🔲
Tithe Meadow *KEMP* RG22 .... 54 D5 🔲
Tiverton Rd *DEAN* RG23 .... 37 H2
Tobago Cl *CHIN* RG24 .... 27 E3
Toledo Gv *AND* SP10 .... 57 G2
Tollgate Cl *DEAN* RG23 .... 36 A4
Tollgate Rd *AND* SP10 .... 57 E5
Tollway *CHIN* RG24 .... 28 B1
Tomlins Cl *TADY* RG26 .... 5 E4
The Topiary *CHIN* RG24 .... 28 B4
Totters La *HTWY* RG27 .... 31 H1
Tower St *ALTN* GU34 .... 58 C5
Town Mill La *WHCH* RG28 .... 47 G5
Townsend Cl *BSTK* RG21 .... 2 B5
Trefoil Cl *HTWY* RG27 .... 22 A2
Trellis Dr *CHIN* RG24 .... 28 B4
Trent Wy *BSTK* RG21 .... 3 K4
Trinidad Cl *CHIN* RG24 .... 27 E3
Trust Cl *HTWY* RG27 .... 30 B1 🔲
Tubb's La *TADY* RG26 .... 17 F1
Tudor Wy *FLET* GU13 .... 45 G3
Tulip Cl *KEMP* RG22 .... 54 B3
Tunworth Ms *TADY* RG26 .... 5 F3
Tunworth Rd *OVTN* RG25 .... 41 F3
Turbary Gdns *TADY* RG26 .... 5 E2
Turk St *ALTN* GU34 .... 58 D4
Turner Cl *BSTK* RG21 .... 39 H3
Turner's Green La *HTWY* RG27 .... 25 F5
Turnpike Wy *DEAN* RG23 .... 35 H5
Tweedsmuir Cl *KEMP* RG22 .... 37 G3
Tweseldown Rd *FLET* GU13 .... 45 H3
Twisell Thorne *FLET* GU13 .... 45 E3
Two Gate La *OVTN* RG25 .... 50 A3
Two Gate Meadow *OVTN* RG25 .... 50 A3

Tyfield *CHIN* RG24 .... 26 B1
Tyne Ct *AND* SP10 .... 57 H1 ▢

U

Union La *KSCL* RG20 .... 9 G3
Upfallow *CHIN* RG24 .... 28 B5
Upper Chestnut Dr *BSTK* RG21 ..... 2 A7
Upper Dro *AND* SP10 .... 56 A3
Upper Farm Rd *DEAN* RG23 .... 52 D2
Upper Grove Rd *ALTN* GU34 .... 58 D5
Upper Neatham Mill La
    ALTN 59 G1
Upper Sherborne Rd *BSTK* RG21 .. 26 D5
Upper St *FLET* GU13 .... 33 F3
Upron Field Cl *KEMP* RG22 .... 54 C3
Upton Crs *BSTK* RG21 .... 26 D5

V

Valencia Wy *AND* SP10 .... 57 F2
The Vale *DEAN* RG23 .... 52 D1
Valley Wy *TADY* RG26 .... 5 H2
Valmeade Cl *HTWY* RG27 .... 30 D1 ▢
Vanburgh Gdns *KEMP* RG22......... 54 C3
Van Dyck Cl *BSTK* RG21 .... 39 H4
Vaughans *ALTN* GU34 .... 59 E4
Velmead Rd *FLET* GU13 .... 33 H5
Velmead Rd *FLET* GU13 .... 33 G5
Verdi Cl *KEMP* RG22 .... 55 E2
The Verne *FLET* GU13 .... 33 H5
Veronica Cl *KEMP* RG22 .... 54 B3
Veronica Dr *FLET* GU13 .... 44 D2
Vespasian Gdns *CHIN* RG24 .... 25 H4
Vestry Cl *AND* SP10 .... 56 D3
Vetch Flds *HTWY* RG27 .... 31 E1
Vicarage Gdns *FLET* GU13 .... 45 F3
Vicarage Hl *ALTN* GU34 .... 58 D4
    HTWY RG27 .... 22 B4
Vicarage Rd *ALTN* GU34.............. 58 C5
Victoria Ct *AND* SP10 .... 56 D4 ▢
Victoria Hill Rd *FLET* GU13 .... 33 E3
Victoria Rd *ALTN* GU34 .... 58 D3
    FLET GU13 .... 33 E3
Victoria Rd East *ALTN* GU34 ...... 59 E3
Victoria St *BSTK* RG21 .... 2 E5
Victory Rbt *BSTK* RG21 .... 2 D3
Vigo Rd *AND* SP10 .... 57 G3
Vincent Dr *AND* SP10................. 57 F4
Vine Tree Cl *TADY* RG26 .... 5 C4
Vinns La *OVTN* RG25................. 49 G3
Violet Cl *KEMP* RG22 .... 54 B3
Vivaldi Cl *KEMP* RG22 .... 55 F3
Vivian Cl *FLET* GU13 .... 45 H1
Vivian Rd *BSTK* RG21 .... 27 F5
Vyne Cl *ALTN* GU34 .... 58 D2 ▢
Vyne Meadow *CHIN* RG24.......... 18 C5
Vyne Rd *BSTK* RG21 .... 2 E1
    CHIN RG24 .... 18 C5

W

Wade Rd *CHIN* RG24 .... 27 H4
Wagner Cl *KEMP* RG22 .... 55 F2
Wakeford Cl *TADY* RG26 .... 5 H2 ▢
Wakefords Copse *FLET* GU13 ...... 45 H4

Wakefords Pk *FLET* GU13 .... 45 H4
Walled Meadow *AND* SP10 .... 57 F4 ▢
Wallins Copse *CHIN* RG24 .... 28 A2 ▢
Wallis Rd *BSTK* RG21 .... 2 E7
Wall La *THLE* RG7 .... 6 D1
Wallop Dr *KEMP* RG22 .... 54 B4
Walnut Cl *ALTN* GU34 .... 58 D2
Walnut Tree Rd *AND* SP10 .... 56 D4
Waltham Ct *OVTN* RG25 .... 50 A2 ▢
Waltham La *OVTN* RG25 .... 50 C5
Waltham St *OVTN* RG25 .... 50 A3
Warbleton Rd *CHIN* RG24 .... 28 B1 ▢
Warblington Cl *TADY* RG26 .... 5 F4
Ward Cl *AND* SP10 .... 57 E1
Warner Ct *AND* SP10 .... 56 D3
Warren Cl *FLET* GU13 .... 33 H5
    HTWY RG27 .... 22 B4
The Warren *TADY* RG26 .... 4 A2
Warton Rd *BSTK* RG21 .... 3 G1
Warwick Rd *DEAN* RG23 .... 37 H1
Watch La *WHCH* RG28 .... 48 B1
Water End La *CHIN* RG24 .... 29 C5
Wateridge Rd *BSTK* RG21 .... 27 F4
Waterlily Cl *BSTK* RG21 .... 3 K4
Waterloo Av *DEAN* RG23 .... 25 H5
Waterloo Ct *AND* SP10 .... 57 E3
Watermills Cl *AND* SP10 .... 56 D5
Water Rede *FLET* GU13 .... 45 E4
Water Ridges *DEAN* RG23 .... 53 E2
Waterside Ct *ALTN* GU34 .... 59 E3 ▢
    FARN GU14 .... 33 H1
Water Wy *BSTK* RG21................. 3 K3
Watery La *AND* SP10 .... 57 F2
    FLET GU13 .... 45 E4
Watling End *KEMP* RG22 .... 54 C3
Watson Acre *AND* SP10 .... 56 C3
Watson Wy *DEAN* RG23 .... 26 A5
Watt Cl *AND* SP10 .... 56 A2
Wavell Cl *KEMP* RG22 .... 38 B5
Waverley Av *BSTK* RG21 .... 38 D5
    FLET GU13 .... 33 F1
Waverley Cl *ODIM* RG29 .... 43 H2
Wayside Rd *DEAN* RG23 .... 37 G2
Weatherby Gdns *HTWY* RG27 .... 22 B3 ▢
Weavers Cl *AND* SP10 .... 57 F3
Webb Cl *CHIN* RG24 .... 27 H2
Weldon Cl *FLET* GU13 .... 45 H2
Wella Rd *KEMP* RG22 .... 38 C5
Wellesley Rd *AND* SP10 .... 57 E5
Wellington Av *FLET* GU13 .... 33 H2
Wellington Crs *TADY* RG26 .... 4 A2
Wellington Rd *AND* SP10 .... 56 D2
Wellington Ter *DEAN* RG23 .... 25 H5
Wellmans Meadow *KSCL* RG20 .... 9 F3
Welton Ct *BSTK* RG21 .... 2 A5
Wensley Dr *FLET* GU13 .... 33 G1 ▢
Wentworth Gdns *ALTN* GU34 ...... 58 C3
Wessex Av *ODIM* RG29 .... 43 F4
Wessex Cl *BSTK* RG21 .... 38 D4
Wessex Crs *ODIM* RG29 .... 43 F4
Wessex Dr *ODIM* RG29 .... 43 F4
Wessex Gdns *AND* SP10 .... 56 D3
West Brook Cl *DEAN* RG23 .... 53 E2
Westbrooke Cl *AND* SP10 .... 57 E4
Westbrooke Rd *ALTN* GU34 .... 58 C4
Westdean Ct *BSTK* RG21 .... 2 B5
Westdeane Ct *BSTK* RG21 .... 2 B5
West End *TADY* RG26 .... 18 A4
Western Av *AND* SP10 .... 57 E4
Western La *ODIM* RG29 .... 43 F3
Western Rd *AND* SP10 .... 57 E4
Western Wy *KEMP* RG22 .... 38 A5
West Field Cl *TADY* RG26............. 5 G3

Westfield Rd *BSTK* RG21 .... 39 F4
West Ham Cl *KEMP* RG22 .... 37 H3
West Ham La *KEMP* RG22 .... 37 G3
Westlyn Rd *TADY* RG26 .... 5 H2
Westminster Cl *FLET* GU13 ...... 33 G2 ▢
    KEMP RG22........................ 54 C3 ▢
Westover Rd *FLET* GU13 .... 33 H3
Westray Cl *BSTK* RG21 .... 27 F5
Westside Cl *AND* SP10 .... 38 A4 ▢
West St *AND* SP10 .... 57 E3 ▢
    ODIM RG29 .... 43 E3
    TADY RG26 .... 5 G3
Wetherby Gdns *AND* SP10 .... 56 C1
Weybrook Ct *TADY* RG26 .... 18 A5
Weyhill Cl *TADY* RG26................. 5 E4
Weyhill Rd *AND* SP10 .... 56 D4
Weysprings Cl *BSTK* RG21 .... 3 J5
Wheeler Hl *HTWY* RG27 .... 31 E1
Whinchat Cl *HTWY* RG27 .... 22 A2
Whin Holt *FLET* GU13 .... 45 G1
Whistler Cl *BSTK* RG21 .... 3 J7
Whistlers La *THLE* RG7 .... 6 C2
Whitedown *ALTN* GU34 .... 58 C5
Whitedown La *ALTN* GU34 .... 58 A5
Whitedown Rd *TADY* RG26 .... 4 C3
White Hart La *BSTK* RG21 .... 3 G5
    TADY RG26 .... 16 D1
Whitehead Cl *CHIN* RG24 .... 28 A5 ▢
White Hl *KSCL* RG20 .... 8 A3
White House Cl *KEMP* RG22 ...... 38 A5
White La *TADY* RG26 .... 34 D1
Whites Cl *HTWY* RG27 .... 30 B1 ▢
Whitestones *KEMP* RG22 .... 54 D4 ▢
Whitewater Rd *ODIM* RG29 .... 43 E1
Whitewood *CHIN* RG24 .... 28 A1
Whitmarsh La *CHIN* RG24 .... 28 C1
Whitney Rd *CHIN* RG24 .... 27 H5
Whynot La *AND* SP10 .... 56 C5
Wickham Cl *ALTN* GU34 .... 58 B5
    FLET GU13 .... 45 E2
    TADY RG26 .... 5 E3
Wickham Pl *FLET* GU13 .... 45 E1
Wickham Rd *FLET* GU13 .... 45 E1
Wicklow Cl *KEMP* RG22 .... 37 G4
Widgeons *ALTN* GU34 .... 58 D2
Widmore Rd *KEMP* RG22 .... 37 H5
Wights Wk *KEMP* RG22 .... 54 C3 ▢
Wigmore Rd *TADY* RG26 .... 4 C2
Wild Herons *HTWY* RG27 .... 31 E1 ▢
Wildmoor La *HTWY* RG27 .... 20 D5
Will Hall Cl *ALTN* GU34 .... 58 B5
William Wy *ALTN* GU34 .... 59 E2 ▢
Willoughby Cl *ALTN* GU34 .... 58 C3
Willoughby Wy *DEAN* RG23 ...... 38 A1
Willow Gv *AND* SP10 .... 56 D4
Willow Rd *TADY* RG26 .... 5 E3
The Willows *AND* SP10 .... 56 D5 ▢
Willow Wy *DEAN* RG23 .... 26 A5
Wilmott Wy *DEAN* RG23 .... 38 A1
Wilsom Cl *ALTN* GU34 .... 59 E4
Wilsom Rd *ALTN* GU34 .... 59 F4
Wilton Pl *BSTK* RG21 .... 2 B4
Wincanton Cl *ALTN* GU34 .... 59 E5
Winchcombe Cl *FLET* GU13 .... 33 G3
Winchcombe Rd *BSTK* RG21 ...... 2 C5
Winchester Gdns *AND* SP10 ...... 57 E5
Winchester Rd *KEMP* RG22 .... 54 B3
Winchester St *AND* SP10 .... 57 F4 ▢
    BSTK RG21 .... 2 E5
    OVTN RG25 .... 50 A2
Winchfield Ct *HTWY* RG27 ...... 32 A3 ▢
Windermere Av *KEMP* RG22....... 37 F5
Windmill Hl *ALTN* GU34 .... 59 E5

Windsor Cl *ALTN* GU34 .... 58 B4 ▢
Windsor Gdns *KEMP* RG22 .... 54 B4
Windsor Pk *ALTN* GU34 .... 58 D5
Windsor Rd *AND* SP10 .... 56 D3
Winklebury Wy *DEAN* RG23 ...... 37 G2
Winkworth La *THLE* RG7 .... 5 F1
Winston Av *TADY* RG26 .... 18 A5
Winterdyne Ms *AND* SP10 .... 56 D4
Winterthur Wy *BSTK* RG21 .... 2 D3
Winton Cha *AND* SP10 .... 57 H3
Wisley Rd *AND* SP10 .... 56 B4
Witan Ct *WHCH* RG28 .... 47 E4
Wither Ri *DEAN* RG23 .... 35 H5
Wolversdene Cl *AND* SP10 ...... 57 G4 ▢
Wolversdene Gdns *AND* SP10 .... 57 G4
Wolversdene Rd *AND* SP10 .... 57 F4
Wolverton La *TADY* RG26 .... 11 E5
Wolverton Rd *TADY* RG26 .... 10 D4
Woodbury Rd *KEMP* RG22 .... 54 C4
Woodcot Cl *KEMP* RG22 .... 54 C4
Woodcote Gn *FLET* GU13 .... 32 D4
Woodgarston Dr *KEMP* RG22 ..... 54 B4
Woodland Ri *FLET* GU13 .... 45 E2
Woodlands *CHIN* RG24 .... 20 B5 ▢
    FLET GU13 .... 33 F2
    OVTN RG25 .... 49 H2
Woodlands Rd *TADY* RG26 .... 4 A2
Woodlands Wy *AND* SP10 .... 57 C5
Woodleigh *FLET* GU13 .... 33 C4
Woodmere Cft *KEMP* RG22 .... 54 A3
Woodpecker Cl *KEMP* RG22 ...... 54 A2
Woodroffe Dr *KEMP* RG22 .... 54 C4
Woodside Gdns *CHIN* RG24 ...... 20 A5
Woods La *OVTN* RG25 .... 55 C5
Wooldridge Crs *ODIM* RG29 ...... 43 E5
Woolford Wy *DEAN* RG23 .... 38 A1
Wool Gv *AND* SP10 .... 57 G4
Wooteys Wy *ALTN* GU34 .... 58 D2
Worcester Av *KEMP* RG22 .... 54 C2
Wordsworth Cl *CHIN* RG24 .... 27 F4
Worting Rd *BSTK* RG21 .... 2 B5
    DEAN RG23 .... 36 D3
    KEMP RG22 .... 38 A3
Wote St *BSTK* RG21 .... 3 F5
Wrekin Cl *KEMP* RG22 .... 37 G4
Wren Cl *ALTN* GU34 .... 59 E2
Wye Ct *AND* SP10 .... 57 G1
Wykeham Ct *ODIM* RG29 .... 43 F5
Wykeham Dr *DEAN* RG23 .... 37 F5
Wyndham Rd *AND* SP10 .... 56 D4 ▢
Wynne Gdns *FLET* GU13 .... 45 H2

Y

Yellowhammer Rd *KEMP* RG22 .... 54 A4
Yellowhammers *ALTN* GU34....... 58 D1
Yew Cl *KSCL* RG20 .... 9 H4
Yew Tree Cl *DEAN* RG23 .... 53 E2
York Cl *KEMP* RG22 .... 54 C2
York La *HTWY* RG27 .... 22 A4
York Ms *ALTN* GU34 .... 59 E3
Youngs Rd *ALTN* GU34 .... 58 D3

Z

Zinnia Cl *KEMP* RG22 .... 54 B4

Index - featured places

The AA - Fanum House
    BSTK RG21 .... 3 K2
Adelaide Medical Centre
    AND SP10 .... 57 F3
Allen Gallery
    ALTN GU34 .... 58 D4
All Saints C of E Junior School
    FLET GU13 .... 32 D4
Alton Business Centre
    ALTN GU34 .... 59 E4
Alton College
    ALTN GU34 .... 58 D2
Alton Convent School
    ALTN GU34 .... 59 E1
Alton County Infant School
    ALTN GU34 .... 59 E3
Alton Health Centre
    ALTN GU34 .... 59 E3
Alton Rugby Club
    ALTN GU34 .... 59 E1

Alton Town Football Club
    ALTN GU34 .... 59 E2
Amery Hill Secondary School
    ALTN GU34 .... 58 D3
Andover Football Club
    AND SP10 .... 56 A1
Andover Golf Club
    AND SP10 .... 57 E5
Andover Museum & the
    Museum of the Iron Age
    AND SP10 .... 57 F3
Andrews Endowed
    Primary School
    ALTN GU34 .... 59 G1
Anstey County Junior School
    ALTN GU34 .... 58 D3
Anton County Infant School
    AND SP10 .... 57 E5
Anton County Junior School
    AND SP10 .... 57 E5

Anton Trading Estate
    AND SP10 .... 56 D5
The Anvil Concert Hall
    BSTK RG21 .... 2 E3
Balksbury County Infant School
    AND SP10 .... 56 B4
Bartley Wood Business Park
    HTWY RG27 .... 31 E2
Basing County Infants School
    CHIN RG24 .... 40 C1
Basingstoke Business Centre
    KEMP RG22 .... 38 B5
Basingstoke College of
    Technology
    BSTK RG21 .... 2 C4
Basingstoke County Court
    BSTK RG21 .... 3 H3
Basingstoke & Deane
    Borough Council
    CHIN RG24 .... 27 H4

Basingstoke Ice Rink
    KEMP RG22 .... 38 A2
Basingstoke & North Hants
    Cricket Club
    BSTK RG21 .... 2 E7
Basingstoke Rugby Club
    KEMP RG22 .... 54 C1
Basingstoke Sports Centre
    BSTK RG21 .... 2 E3
Basingstoke Town
    Football Club
    KEMP RG22 .... 38 B5
Beech Down County
    Primary School
    KEMP RG22 .... 55 E2
Bilton Industrial Estate
    CHIN RG24 .... 27 G3
Bishop Challoner RC
    Secondary School
    KEMP RG22 .... 37 H4

Bishopswood Co Junior School
  TADY RG26 .... 5 E3
Bishopwood Co Infant School
  TADY RG26 .... 5 E4
Breakers Ten Pin Bowl & Snooker
  Centre
  AND SP10 .... 57 E4
Brick Kiln Industrial Estate
  TADY RG26 .... 5 E2
Brighton Hill Community School
  KEMP RG22 .... 55 E1
Burnham Copse Junior School
  TADY RG26 .... 4 D2
Burnside Surgery
  FLET GU13 .... 33 G3
Buryfields Infant School
  ODIM RG29 .... 43 G3
The Business Centre
  BSTK RG21 .... 3 G4
The Butts County
  Primary School *ALTN* GU34 ...... 58 B5
Calleva Roman Antiquity and
  Museum
  THLE RG7 .... 6 C2
Calthorpe Park School
  FLET GU13 .... 32 C4
Castle Hill Junior School
  DEAN RG23 .... 37 G2
Century Galleries
  HTWY RG27 .... 22 B3
Chalkridge School
  KEMP RG22 .... 55 F1
Chantry Centre Shopping
  Precinct
  AND SP10 .... 57 E3
Charlton Hill Surgery
  AND SP10 .... 56 C2
Charlton Road Health Centre
  AND SP10 .... 56 C2
Chineham Park Primary School
  CHIN RG24 .... 27 G4
Church Grange & Bramblys
  Grange Health Centre
  BSTK RG21 .... 2 D5
Church Grange Lychpit Surgery
  CHIN RG24 .... 28 A5
Church of England
  Primary School
  AND SP10 .... 57 F4
Cliddesden Primary School
  OVTN RG25 .... 55 H5
Clift Surgery
  TADY RG26 .... 15 H2
Court Moor School
  FLET GU13 .... 33 F5
Coxmoor Farm Light
  Industrial Estate
  NFNM GU10 .... 44 B5
Cranbourne Secondary School
  BSTK RG21 .... 38 C4
Cricklade Theatre
  AND SP10 .... 57 E3
Crookham C of E Infants School
  FLET GU13 .... 45 F3
Crookham County Junior School
  FLET GU13 .... 45 H3
Curtis Museum
  ALTN GU34 .... 58 D3
Daneshill East Industrial Estate
  CHIN RG24 .... 39 H1
Daneshill Industrial Estate
  CHIN RG24 .... 27 H5
Diva Gallery
  ODIM RG29 .... 43 G2
Dogmersfield C of E
  Primary School
  HTWY RG27 .... 32 A5
Dove House School
  BSTK RG21 .... 27 E5
East Barn Surgery
  CHIN RG24 .... 28 A4
Eggars School
  ALTN GU34 .... 59 F1
Evingar Industrial Estate
  WHCH RG28 .... 47 E4
Fairfields Primary School
  BSTK RG21 .... 2 E6
Finns Industrial Park
  NFNM GU10 .... 44 B5
Fleet Business Park
  FLET GU13 .... 45 H4
Fleet Community Hospital
  FLET GU13 .... 33 E2
Fleet Police Station
  FLET GU13 .... 33 F4

Focus 303 Business Centre
  AND SP10 .... 57 H2
Fort Hill School
  DEAN RG23 .... 37 H1
Forthill Surgery
  DEAN RG23 .... 37 H1
Gillies Health Centre
  KEMP RG22 .... 55 E2
Greenfields Junior School
  HTWY RG27 .... 22 A4
Grey House Private School
  HTWY RG27 .... 22 B3
The Hampshire Clinic
  CHIN RG24 .... 39 H1
Hampshire County Council
  BSTK RG21 .... 3 F4
Hampshire County Council
  - Basing House
  CHIN RG24 .... 40 B1
Hampshire County Council
  - Chute House
  BSTK RG21 .... 2 E3
Harriet Costello School
  BSTK RG21 .... 3 H5
Harrow Way Community School
  AND SP10 .... 56 B1
Hart Sports Centre
  FLET GU13 .... 32 C4
Hassocks Wood Industrial Estate
  CHIN RG24 .... 27 H5
Hatch Warren County
  Infant School
  KEMP RG22 .... 54 D3
Hatch Warren County
  Junior School
  KEMP RG22 .... 54 D3
Hatch Warren Retail Park
  KEMP RG22 .... 54 B4
Hatch Warren Surgery
  KEMP RG22 .... 54 B4
The Hawthorns School
  KEMP RG22 .... 54 D1
Haymarket Theatre
  BSTK RG21 .... 2 E5
Holmwood Health Centre
  TADY RG26 .... 4 D2
Holybourne Theatre
  ALTN GU34 .... 59 G1
Hook County Junior School
  HTWY RG27 .... 30 D1
Hook Infant School
  HTWY RG27 .... 30 D1
Houndmills Industrial Estate
  BSTK RG21 .... 26 B5
The Hurst Community School
  TADY RG26 .... 4 A2
Ian Walker Odiham Gallery
  ODIM RG29 .... 43 G2
Icknield School
  AND SP10 .... 57 H1
John Hanson Community School
  AND SP10 .... 56 C4
John Hunt of Everest
  Community School
  CHIN RG24 .... 27 F3
Kempshott County
  Infant School
  KEMP RG22 .... 54 B2
Kempshott County
  Junior School
  KEMP RG22 .... 54 B2
The Kerridge Industrial Estate
  ALTN GU34 .... 59 E3
Kingsclere Health Centre
  KSCL RG20 .... 9 G4
Kingsclere Primary School
  KSCL RG20 .... 9 G4
Kings Furlong Infant School
  BSTK RG21 .... 2 A7
Kings Furlong Junior School
  BSTK RG21 .... 2 B7
Kings School
  BSTK RG21 .... 2 D5
Leisure Centre
  AND SP10 .... 57 E3
Limington House School
  KEMP RG22 .... 38 A4
Loddon Business Centre
  CHIN RG24 .... 28 A5
London Road School
  ODIM RG29 .... 43 G2
Longfellow Parade Clinic
  CHIN RG24 .... 27 F4
The Malls/the Walks
  Shopping Centre
  BSTK RG21 .... 3 F3

Manorfield Infant School
  KEMP RG22 .... 55 F3
The Manse Health Centre
  AND SP10 .... 57 F3
Maple Ridge School
  BSTK RG21 .... 26 D5
Mark Way School
  AND SP10 .... 57 G3
Marnel Infant & Junior Schools
  CHIN RG24 .... 27 F3
Mayfield School
  ALTN GU34 .... 59 F2
Mayhill County Junior School
  ODIM RG29 .... 43 G3
May's Bounty
  BSTK RG21 .... 2 E7
Merton County Junior School
  CHIN RG24 .... 26 D4
Milestone Transport Museum
  KEMP RG22 .... 37 H2
Morland Surgery
  TADY RG26 .... 5 E4
Mylen Business Centre
  AND SP10 .... 56 C3
Newbury District Council
  WHCH RG28 .... 47 F4
The New Chineham Surgery
  CHIN RG24 .... 28 A2
North Hampshire Hospital
  CHIN RG24 .... 26 B4
Oakley C of E Junior School
  DEAN RG23 .... 52 D1
Oakley County Infant School
  DEAN RG23 .... 52 D1
Oakridge County Junior School
  BSTK RG21 .... 26 D5
Oakwood School
  HTWY RG27 .... 22 B4
Odiham Castle
  ODIM RG29 .... 42 D1
Odiham Cottage Hospital
  ODIM RG29 .... 43 G3
The Odiham Health Centre
  ODIM RG29 .... 43 F2
Old Basing Surgery
  CHIN RG24 .... 40 C2
The Omni Business Centre
  ALTN GU34 .... 59 F4
Oriel Business Park
  ALTN GU34 .... 59 F4
Osborn Way Industrial Estate
  HTWY RG27 .... 30 C2
Overbridge Surgery
  KEMP RG22 .... 38 B3
Overton C of E Primary School
  OVTN RG25 .... 49 G1
Overton Gallery
  OVTN RG25 .... 49 H2
Overton Surgery
  OVTN RG25 .... 50 A2
Park View Infant School
  KEMP RG22 .... 37 H5
Park View Junior School
  KEMP RG22 .... 37 H4
Portway Junior School
  AND SP10 .... 56 A3
The Priory Primary School
  TADY RG26 .... 13 G5
Queen Marys College
  BSTK RG21 .... 39 E4
Redfields Industrial Estate
  FLET GU13 .... 45 F4
Redfields Industrial Park
  FLET GU13 .... 45 E5
Richard Aldworth
  Community School
  KEMP RG22 .... 38 A5
Richmond Surgery
  FLET GU13 .... 45 F1
Riverwey Industrial Park
  ALTN GU34 .... 59 F3
Robert Mays School
  ODIM RG29 .... 43 E2
Ruckstall County
  Primary School
  BSTK RG21 .... 3 J7
St Annes Catholic
  Primary School
  KEMP RG22 .... 38 A4
St Bedes Catholic
  Primary School
  CHIN RG24 .... 26 D3
St Johns School
  BSTK RG21 .... 38 D4

St John the Baptist RC
  Primary School
  AND SP10 .... 56 B4
St Lawrence C of E (Controlled)
  Primary School
  ALTN GU34 .... 58 C3
St Marks Primary School
  KEMP RG22 .... 54 C4
St Marys C of E Junior School
  CHIN RG24 .... 40 C1
St Marys Surgery
  AND SP10 .... 57 F3
St Nicholas School
  NFNM GU10 .... 45 E5
Sandford Springs Golf Club
  TADY RG26 .... 10 B4
Saxonwood School for the
  Handicapped
  DEAN RG23 .... 25 G4
Sherborne St John
  Primary School *CHIN* RG24 ...... 18 B5
Silchester Primary School
  THLE RG7 .... 6 C2
South Ham Medical Centre
  KEMP RG22 .... 37 H4
Station Industrial Estate
  FLET GU13 .... 33 H1
Superstore
  BSTK RG21 .... 2 A4
The Surgery
  DEAN RG23 .... 53 E2
Surrey Hampshire Borders
  Nhs Trust
  BSTK RG21 .... 3 G4
Tadley Cp School
  TADY RG26 .... 5 F5
Tadley Police Station
  TADY RG26 .... 5 E2
Tavistock County Infant School
  FLET GU13 .... 32 D4
Tempus Business Centre
  BSTK RG21 .... 26 C5
Tennis Club
  FLET GU13 .... 45 F4
Thorneycroft Industrial Estate
  BSTK RG21 .... 2 A5
Tweseldown Infant School
  FLET GU13 .... 45 H3
Viables Industrial Estate
  KEMP RG22 .... 55 G2
Vickers Business Centre
  CHIN RG24 .... 26 B4
Vigo County Infant School
  AND SP10 .... 57 G2
Vigo County Junior School
  AND SP10 .... 57 G2
War Memorial Hospital
  AND SP10 .... 56 C1
Wellum House Dental
  Health Centre
  AND SP10 .... 57 E4
Wessex Bowl
  KEMP RG22 .... 37 H2
West March Business Centre
  AND SP10 .... 57 E1
Whitedown Special School
  ALTN GU34 .... 58 C5
White Hart Gallery
  OVTN RG25 .... 49 H2
Willis Museum
  BSTK RG21 .... 3 F5
Willowdene Play School
  CHIN RG24 .... 28 A2
Winchester Road
  Industrial Estate
  BSTK RG21 .... 38 C4
Winklebury Infant School
  DEAN RG23 .... 38 A1
Winklebury Junior School
  DEAN RG23 .... 38 A1
Winklebury Medical Centre
  DEAN RG23 .... 37 H1
Winton Play School
  AND SP10 .... 57 F3
The Winton School
  AND SP10 .... 57 H3
Wolverdene School
  AND SP10 .... 57 F4
Worldham Park Golf Club
  ALTN GU34 .... 59 G5
Worting County Infant School
  DEAN RG23 .... 37 F3
Worting County Junior School
  KEMP RG22 .... 37 G3